MOMENTS OF
SERENDIPITY

Elizabeth Dettling Moreno

ACKNOWLEDGEMENTS

This book of inspirations is a hodgepodge of musings that I've had over the past few years. Most of these essays were originally published in **The Wharton Journal-Spectator** or in the online edition of **Katy Christian Magazine**. Many readers, including classmates from years gone by, commented on the content and asked if I was going to publish anything else. This book is my response to their kind and encouraging feedback.

May God bless you with understanding as you read these nuggets of truth.

Copyright © 2025 Elizabeth Moreno

All rights reserved. No part of this publication may be reproduced, distributed, or transmitted in any form or by any means, including photocopying, recording, or other electronic or mechanical methods, without the prior written permission of the publisher, except in the case of brief quotations embodied in critical reviews and certain other noncommercial uses permitted by copyright law.

Print ISBN: 978-1-63616-245-4
eBook ISBN: 978-1-63616-246-1

Published By Opportune Independent Publishing Co.

Printed in the United States of America

Cover image photo by John Dettling, Jr.

For permission requests, please email the publisher with the subject line as "Attention: Permissions Coordinator" to the email address below:
Info@Opportunepublishing.com

All Bible verses used in this book are from the King James Version, unless otherwise stated.

Dedicated to
My husband
Randy Jay Tolman.
I am so glad
That God told you
To take care of me, Elizabeth,
In our twilight years.
You are a blessing
And I love you!

ENDORSEMENTS

Through the years, Liz's writings have brought enlightened and joy-filled encouragement to her readers. Whether via children's books, newspaper columns, or simply encouraging text messages, Liz has used God's gift of writing to His glory and the uplifting of her readers, me included. This new work will be another blessing to all who read it.

—Jane D. Bard, Friend and Fan

A heartfelt, unique perspective of real-life experiences that will resonate with readers. Liz finds lessons to learn in each of life's events, especially when God is invited into the circumstances

—Lillian Carolan

I have had the privilege of reading all of Liz's books and I must say that each one of them brings a new and very special perspective on life here and in eternity. Liz is an awesomely gifted author with spiritual insights that reach far beyond the paper and ink of her books. I am sure all who read her latest book will whole-heartily agree that God has anointed and blessed Liz with this talent for such a time as this. May God bless you as you feast upon this new creation from His faithful servant.

—Bishop Randy J. Tolman
Elizabeth's husband

It is an honor to endorse my dear friend, Elizabeth, for her latest book, Moments of Serendipity. As a gifted writer and editor, she has a rare ability to express deep truths with openness, vulnerability, and humor. Her words invite readers to reflect, find joy, and embrace the unexpected moments of grace in life.

I wholeheartedly recommend **Moments of Serendipity** *and the woman behind it. She is not just a talented writer—she is a remarkable person whose wisdom and kindness shine through everything she does.*

—Dr. Isabel Yanez, D.Min

TABLE OF CONTENTS

1. God Can Restore – Even Money — 10
2. Trusting God — 13
3. Is It Better to Give Than Receive? — 15
4. The Mindlessness of Going in Circles — 17
5. Changing the Channel in my Mind — 19
6. Animals Help People — 21
7. Israel at Christmas Time — 24
8. Dancing Flowers offer Praise — 27
9. A Christmas Love Letter — 30
10. But God… — 33
11. The Rose That Would not Die — 36
12. Do You See Me? — 38
13. Fear Not — 41
14. What Tool Are You? — 43
15. Displaced Faith — 45
16. Self-Made Man? Not Likely! — 47
17. The Favor of God — 50
18. Debunking Old Wives Tales — 53
19. They are With Us Still — 56
20. The Joy of Little Victories — 59
21. All Parts Work Together — 62
22. The Audacity of Youth — 65
23. Power of Persistent Prayer — 67

24. That Still, Small Voice	70
25. Roots of Thankfulness	73
26. Redeeming the Trash	75
27. The Blessing of a New Beginning	78
28. The Ritual of Clean Sheets	80
29. Locked Doors Lead to Trust	82
30. Use up, Repair, Make Do, or Do Without	85
31. The Futility of Vanity	87
32. It All Depends on your Perspective	90
33. In the Light of Eternity	92
34. Happy Being Me	94
35. You Can't Judge a Book by its Cover	96
36. The Miracle of the Tithe	99
37. I Remember Going Back to College	102
38. Looking at Life from God's Perspective	105
39. Synchronized Flying and Other Marvels of Nature	107
40. From my Head to my Heart	110
About the Author	113

GOD CAN RESTORE – EVEN MONEY
(God's Provision)

    A long time ago, there was a king who hired soldiers from another country to fight a battle for his kingdom. He went to great expense to hire those mercenaries to work for him. However, before the battle began, a prophet told him that he should not go to war and that he should let the soldiers return to their homes.
    The king, whose name was Amaziah, was confused because he had already spent 100 silver talents, or, in today's vernacular, millions of dollars, to buy their services and now he was told to just let the money go and that it would be restored to him, but not to go to battle.
    You can read the story for yourself in the Bible, 2 Chronicles 25:9.
    Amaziah listened to the man of God and did not use the hired army to go to war. Instead, he used the citizens of his country and they came out triumphant.
    If you are like Amaziah, you have undoubtedly felt like you have poured money down a drain and you wondered how you could recoup loss.
    Maybe you bought a car that turned out to be a lemon (guilty). Maybe you got talked into a "special deal just for you" at a store, or online, or even in a foreign country. (Guilty again). Maybe some smooth-talking salesman convinced you to buy something that you might have been able to live without but that salesman convinced you how empty your life would be without it. (I hate to admit guilt on this one too!)
    Looking back, it is so easy to see the mistakes after the facts. At the time, though, it was very difficult to see the $$$ those mistakes would end up costing me. However, I

found a silver lining when I read this scripture. It gave me comfort when I realized it was just money--- not something irreplaceable. I had to look for a while, but I did find lessons learned in spite of me.

For one thing, I realized something I should **not** do in future business ventures...make snap decisions on things that are financial choices. For another, I may have been a catalyst to help a sales person make their quota for the day. (I've been in sales and I know the pressure these people work under.) The most important lesson is that I should have consulted the Lord before jumping into those agreements. If I had, and, if I had listened to that still, small Voice, I could have saved myself not just hundreds, but thousands, of dollars.

As long as I've been walking with the Lord, I should have realized the importance of **Psalm 37:23-24**:
> *The steps of a good man are ordered by the L*ORD*: and he delighteth in his way. Though he fall, he shall not be utterly cast down: for the Lord upholdeth him with his hand and he forgives faithfully when I have made a blunder.*

> **Proverbs** 16:9
> *Therefore my heart is glad, and my glory rejoiceth: my flesh also shall rest in hope.*

I believe that and I thank God that His mercies are new every morning.

> **Lamentations** 3:22-23
> *It is of the Lord mercies that we are not consumed, because his compassions fail not. [23] They are new every morning: great is thy faithfulness.*

Maybe you didn't make a financial blunder, but somehow, you feel that life did not turn out as you hoped for...maybe a bad marriage, maybe a baby out of wedlock...maybe ill health...maybe severed relationships...maybe an abortion...maybe (you name it) God is fully aware of your circumstances and He is waiting for you to acknowledge Him and invite Him into your life and all that pertains to it. He will not ignore a sincere heart and He will restore the years the canker worm ate away.

Joel 2:25
And I will restore to you the years that the locust hath eaten, the cankerworm, and the caterpillar, and the palmerworm...

Psalm 27:1
The Lord is my light and my salvation; whom (or what) shall I fear? the Lord is the strength of my life; of whom shall I be afraid?

Bottom line is trust Him—He's got it all under control.

TRUSTING GOD

Sometimes life is a breeze and everything seems to go according to our plans, but sometimes it seems to be a long, hard journey, and we need encouragement along the way. A friend of mine was in that spot recently and needed direction. He craved a word from God because he felt restless in his soul, so he prayed till he got an answer.

According to **Hebrews 11:1**, "Now faith is the substance of things hoped for, the evidence of things not seen." My friend was exhibiting this kind of faith when he prayed his heartfelt prayer. Finally, after a long time on his knees, he got what he called a word from the Lord… "I have not abandoned you!"

Although it wasn't what he was looking for, it was the reassurance that he needed. He was able to continue to walk by faith, in spite of not being able to walk by sight. His problem didn't go away, but he knew he wasn't facing it alone.

Proverbs 3:5-6 says, "Trust in the Lord with all thine heart; and lean not unto thine own understanding. In all thy ways acknowledge Him, and He shall direct thy paths." That's what my friend was doing, but Indian boys have to learn to trust in order to enter manhood in their tribe.

There is a story about how a Cherokee boy is initiated into manhood. The father takes his adolescent child into the woods, blindfolds him, and tells him NOT to take the mask off until the next morning. Then his father leaves him, and the child sits on a tree stump, waiting for daylight.

As he waits, he hears predators close by. He hears screams and howls in the distance. He fears because he believes his very life may be in danger. And yet, he stoically sits, waiting for the sun to rise. He wants to achieve manhood so desperately that he is willing to take whatever risk is needed in order to make the transition from Indian child to Indian brave.

When the morning sun warms his face, the child pulls off the mask and finds that his father has been sitting nearby on another stump all night long. It is then that he realizes he never was abandoned or totally left alone. His father was guarding him without the child even being aware of his presence. The child has become a man and, in the process, has learned to walk by faith.

How like you and me? So often we feel left alone, but if truth be known, we are never without God's care. We may wonder and hesitate to take the next step, but when we do, our Father rewards us. We learn to walk by faith and not by sight.

What we need is to learn to trust and obey, even if we are not sure of where He is leading. Know that God honors faith, and He will take care of His own. If you can learn to trust Him, you will reap the rewards in this life and in the next. Why not start your journey of faith today?

2 Corinthians 5:7
For we walk by faith, not by sight.

Isaiah 26:4
Trust ye in the Lord forever: for in the Lord Jehovah is everlasting strength.

Hebrews 13:5
I will never leave thee, nor forsake thee.

Psalm 56:3–4
What time I am afraid, I will trust in thee. In God I will praise His word, in God I have put my trust; I will not fear what flesh can do unto me.

IS IT BETTER TO GIVE THAN RECEIVE?
(Generosity toward Others)

    When I was a child, I loved getting gifts! No matter if it was my birthday or Christmas or no occasion at all, gifts were indescribably wonderful! Candy, or little toy dolls, or even a small globe—the gift made me a happy camper.
    I remember one year in particular: I was excited for the coming of Christmas, and I did a little detective work to find out what my gift for that year would be. Being the sleuth that I was, I waited till my mom was gone so I could go climbing around in her closet, searching for my package. Eureka! I found it on the top shelf—it was a beautiful blue blouse with puffy sleeves. I was so proud of myself for being sneaky. But then the guilt set in, and I had to figure out how to act surprised when I actually received my present.
    I'd like to think I learned my lesson that year, but I'm not so sure I did. Although I'm not guilty of sleuthing as I did sixty years ago, as I've matured, I've found that I find greater pleasure in giving rather than receiving.
    To be honest, I have been on the receiving end of Christmas gifts from more than just immediate members of my family. When my kids were little, we were on the list several times for groups like Good Fellows, or Angel Tree, or K.C.'s. The kindnesses we were shown brought plenty of smiles and squeals of delight from my youngsters. They loved the excitement of gifts to open and a plethora of foods. It was a blessing for us to be thought of, but although I was thankful, I would have rather been the giver than the receiver.
    Don't get me wrong—I greatly appreciated all those that helped make the holidays a wonderful time for all of us.

However, I want to be one of those who brings smiles out of others. Something inside me looks for ways to be a giver.

Since that time, I've found that the Bible says that very thing.

Acts 20:35 "... I remembered the words of the Lord Jesus, 'It is more blessed to give than to receive.'"

I do enjoy giving, but I try to give with wisdom. What I really try to do is pass on the kindness—or, as some might say, "play it forward."

Since we have been greatly blessed, I try to bless those organizations that have blessed me and my family. Although most giving is done at Christmastime, giving is not limited by dates on the calendar. For example, many years ago someone bought my son's chickens at the Wharton County Fair and gave him the encouragement he needed. By the next year, our financial situation was greatly improved, and we were in a position to help others in the same way that our son was helped.

I have found that in giving, I find joy. The looks of surprise and appreciation are priceless—especially when the gifts are needed.

I'm not a benevolent fairy godmother, but I do want to share the love of the true God in whatever way I can. I've also found that I can't outgive God. His gifts are the best of all. And He uses other people to accomplish His goals.

Happy giving!

Luke 6:38
Give, and it shall be given unto you; good measure, pressed down, and shaken together, and running over, shall men give into your bosom.

2 Corinthians 9:6
But this I say, He which soweth sparingly shall reap also sparingly; and he which soweth bountifully shall reap also bountifully.

THE MINDLESSNESS OF GOING IN CIRCLES
(calling and purpose)

As I sit at my computer, I look out the window and watch little sparrows go round and round and round on the free-hanging bird feeder. Curiously enough, they seem to enjoy it. Sometimes, they get caught up in the movement, like a person can get caught up in a turnstile for a revolving door. But they hop on and hop off without much effort, and they take the ride several times a day.

When I first realized what the birds were doing, it reminded me of the way hamsters have little wheels in their cages. It seems those wheels are only there to entertain the hamsters. Like the birds, the hamsters go round and round and round. Then I thought about all the energy they put out and have no reward for their efforts.

> **Philippians 2:16**
> *Holding forth the word of life; that I may rejoice in the day of Christ, that I have not run in vain, neither laboured in vain.*

People are so much like the little critters in creation. Children have always loved to ride merry-go-rounds. My friends and I rode them till we could not stand straight—and we always went back for more. The only reward we received for going in circles was a lightheaded feeling and maybe a round of nausea.

Aren't we like this in real life, too? We get caught in the trap of repeating an old habit and expect different outcomes. Society has a saying: "Keep doing what you have been doing, and you will get what you have always been getting." If you are a little sparrow, you get the fun of going in circles. If you are a hamster, you keep getting nowhere by chasing yourself.

Although some things, by their very nature, are repetitious, life doesn't have to be that way. Sometimes people need to step out in faith to broaden their horizons. It takes courage to break old habits. It takes courage to think in a different direction.

It sounds like I'm being very critical of repetitious activity, but there is another side to that coin. The favorable side is that of faithfulness. So many times, we get caught up in the monotony of a task that we forget that there is a reward for consistency. The "same-o, same-o" indicates boredom, but the Lord of All is looking for someone who tries to please Him with their actions.

If you realize that fact and live accordingly, you may qualify for the Master to say unto you—"Well done, my good and faithful servant."

> **Matthew 25:21**
> *His lord said unto him, Well done, thou good and faithful servant: thou hast been faithful over a few things; I will make thee ruler over many things: enter thou into the joy of thy lord.*

CHANGING THE CHANNEL IN MY MIND
(Self Control)

Once upon a time, I worked full time at KANI Country Radio, the small country music station that used to be in Wharton, Texas. It was my job to either cover the local news or sell advertising. As I went about my duties, I usually kept my car radio tuned to the station so I would keep up with whatever was happening on the air. But as I listened to the banter between the disc jockeys, I listened to the music, and a bunch of it wormed its way into my mind.

Before you pass judgment on me for working in such a questionable environment, please know I needed the income. I was a divorcée with four little ones, and this was a job that I was good at. However, it was not the kind of environment that encouraged solid Christian thinking.

Country music has a way of getting a strong picture across with the way it uses words, and it was no different in the late '70s. Before long, I was singing along with "Take This Job and Shove It," or "Jolene," or "Behind Closed Doors," and "Who's Cheating Who?" There were dozens of songs with lyrics that were not conducive to Godly thinking, and it was then that I realized I needed to change the channel in my mind.

It wasn't easy, but I chose to think on other songs and words, even as my mind was assaulted with all the station had to offer. I had to choose to dwell on praise songs and think on things from above rather than banal things of earth.

I intentionally tuned the channel in my mind to realize I had "My Father's Eyes," and "You Light Up My Life," as I sang to the Lord. I remembered to "Put My Hand in the Hand of the Man Who Walked on Water" as I took "One Day at a

Time." Changing the mental channel made it easy to see "The Day He Wore My Crown" and "What a Difference He Made in My Life."

Even though I haven't worked at that station for more than 40 years, I still find myself having to change that channel in my mind. Sometimes it's because of a negative report from a doctor. Sometimes it's because someone has been complaining and I join in concerning whatever perceived misjustice has happened. Sometimes it's because I spend too much time dwelling on the negatives in life rather than the positives.

It's easy to let the prerecorded message saturate my brain, but it takes effort to intentionally change the channel.

Philippians 4:8
Finally, brethren, whatsoever things are true, whatsoever things are honest, whatsoever things are just, whatsoever things are pure, whatsoever things are lovely, whatsoever things are of good report; if there be any virtue, and if there be any praise, think on these things.

2 Corinthians 10:5
Casting down imaginations, and every high thing that exalteth itself against the knowledge of God, and bringing into captivity every thought to the obedience of Christ;

Romans 12:2
And be not conformed to this world: but be ye transformed by the renewing of your mind, that ye may prove what is that good, and acceptable, and perfect, will of God.

ANIMALS HELP PEOPLE
(creation)

Have you ever thought about how animals interact with people? Like Balaam's donkey, who told him about the angel with the sword in the pathway? Or the raven that brought bread and meat to Elijah in the wilderness? Or the rooster in the courtyard who crowed before Peter denied Jesus three times? Or the fish that had coins in its mouth so Peter could pay taxes for both himself and Jesus?

I had that experience recently when our young Akita/Pyrenees mix helped get me out of a real fix.

Because my car was being repaired, I was driving a rental car for a week, and although it was very nice, it was too fancy for my taste. It had a keyless entry fob, but up until that time, I had never heard of a fob, much less seen one in action. Before the week was up, however, I learned how valuable that little device really is.

It was about day 3 of using the rental car when the fob came up MIA. I looked high and low without any success. I even went to the rental company and asked for a temporary replacement fob until I could find the original. The clerk let me know that there were no replacements available and that it would cost $300 to replace it. That rascal was nowhere to be found, but I continued my search in the house, in the yard, between the car seats, and in our other car. Here I had a beautiful car to be driving, but without the fob, I couldn't go anywhere. I called or sent emails to my friends asking for prayer for God's intervention.

A friend of mine reminded me that God was in control and he prayed that the Holy Spirit would reveal the location of the fob. He told me that God knew where it was and that losing it may have been a small lesson about our dependence on God for even small things.

My friend said, "He will show you—do not fret or worry about it. God has this—He has your back." I accepted his prayers, along with all the others being offered on my behalf. I was still flustered, but trusted God and praised Him anyway.

The car was supposed to be turned in on Monday, but by the time Sunday evening came around, I had almost given in to defeat. I knew I was going to spend my hard-earned cash to replace the missing device.

Then my son came home from work and he was fixing to mess with me because I still hadn't found the fob. But, instead, he showed mercy. Just then, Anna, our pup (who already weighed 20 pounds), dropped something black at his feet. He checked it out and, lo and behold, there was the lost fob! I have no idea if she had it hidden all that time or not, but I am definitely praising God for the timing and for having mercy on me. I guess God decided so many people were bombarding Heaven on my behalf, that He said, "She's been in enough misery already... I'll have the dog bring it to her like I had ravens take food to Elijah."

Sometimes people say an animal is just an animal, but I'm here to tell you that animals can be servants of the Most High God, too... maybe not quite like people, but definitely used for His purposes. Needless to say, it was another lesson in depending on God in even the small things, just like my friend said. And God gets all the glory.

1 Kings 17:6
And the ravens brought him bread and flesh in the morning, and bread and flesh in the evening; and he drank of the brook.

Matthew 17:27
Notwithstanding, lest we should offend them, go thou to the sea, and cast an hook, and take up the fish that first

cometh up; and when thou hast opened his mouth, thou shalt find a piece of money: that take, and give unto them for me and thee.

Job 12:7–10
*But ask now the beasts, and they shall teach thee; and the fowls of the air, and they shall tell thee:
Or speak to the earth, and it shall teach thee: and the fishes of the sea shall declare unto thee.
Who knoweth not in all these that the hand of the Lord hath wrought this?
In whose hand is the soul of every living thing, and the breath of all mankind.*

Mark 14:72
And the second time the cock crew. And Peter called to mind the word that Jesus said unto him, Before the cock crow twice, thou shalt deny me thrice. And when he thought thereon, he wept.

ISRAEL AT CHRISTMASTIME
(God's Love)

My husband, Randy, and I took a trip to Israel in 2021 to celebrate our first wedding anniversary, and we were blessed beyond measure to be there at the beginning of one of the holiest seasons of the Christian calendar: Christmas. We were equally blessed to have our own personal tour guides to show us sites that the locals know well. Seeing the land where Jesus walked and trying to follow His footsteps puts the journey in perspective.

Our hosts drove us from the region of Bethlehem to Nazareth in an air-conditioned car. I can't imagine what it was like to travel 70 to 90 miles either walking or riding on a donkey, not even to mention being pregnant. Although Mary and Joseph didn't realize it at the time, their journey was done in order to fulfill prophecy:

> **Micah 5:2**
> *But thou, Bethlehem Ephratah, though thou be little among the thousands of Judah, yet out of thee shall he come forth unto me that is to be ruler in Israel; whose goings forth have been from of old, from everlasting.*

One of the places we made sure to visit was the Church of the Nativity in Bethlehem. Locals say this is the exact location of where the manger was that Jesus was laid in. It wasn't the wooden feed holder that we've come to recognize over the years... it was actually a water trough that was made of a large stone. Even though He came without worldly fanfare, great amounts of gold and silver ornamentation mark the spot. Unless you actually know the Christmas story, you would never know that this was a stall for livestock over two thousand years ago. And yet, the King of Heaven chose this humble dwelling to make His entrance into the world that He spoke into being.

The shepherds' field is within walking distance of the Church of the Nativity. Although there are buildings all around, a few acres on the hillside are left alone with just grass growing. There is a sign at the entrance to the field that tells visitors that they can't enter the field without the permission of a priest who is supposed to be on duty. (We didn't find one.) It's not a big stretch of the imagination to picture a flock of sheep grazing by moonlight as the angel choir sang, "Glory to God." And then, picture the shepherds leaving their sheep and running to the village to find the Baby that the angels had just announced.

> **Luke 2:15**
> *And it came to pass, as the angels were gone away from them into heaven, the shepherds said one to another, Let us now go even unto Bethlehem, and see this thing which is come to pass, which the Lord hath made known unto us.*

Next door to the Church of the Nativity is another shrine… this time, it's all because of drops of milk. Legend says that when Joseph was told by the angel to take Mary and Baby Jesus to Egypt, she needed to nurse Him along the way. While He was nursing, a few drops of her milk fell to the ground, turning the soil white. Generations later, some women go on pilgrimages to the Milk Grotto in Israel, praying for miracles of conception and for them to be able to successfully nurse their own babies.

> **Matthew 2:13**
> *And when they were departed, behold, the angel of the Lord appeareth to Joseph in a dream, saying, Arise, and*

take the young child and his mother, and flee into Egypt, and be thou there until I bring thee word: for Herod will seek the young child to destroy him.

One location that is not commercialized is the re-creation of the Nazareth Village. The Bible tells us that Jesus grew up in Nazareth, and this village is a small replica of His hometown. A few hills where the Child Jesus might have played are near the compound. The village portrays many situations that were part of Jesus' life: the carpenter's shop, the winepress, the sheepfold, the temple, the weaver, the olive press. People who work here are volunteers because they love the Lord and they see value in the lessons that they can help teach in this setting.

Matthew 2:23
… and he came and dwelt in a city called Nazareth: that it might be fulfilled which was spoken by the prophets, He shall be called a Nazarene.

Thank God that Jesus came in the fullness of time, and He came to set the captives free! So many people think of God as high and mighty and unapproachable. Well, He is high and mighty, but He is very approachable because of what Jesus did on our behalf. He is the best present ever, and we are saved because He has called us to be His own.

Galatians 4:4-5 – "… when the fulness of the time was come, God sent forth his Son, made of a woman, made under the law, to redeem them that were under the law, that we might receive the adoption of sons."

May God bless us, everyone!

DANCING FLOWERS OFFER PRAISE
(worship)

Sometimes, I look at my dining room window, and there, on the windowsill, a pretty little red flower dances in the sunshine. Scarlett has a friend right next to her: Vi, a purple posy that dances with her. Sometimes they dance in unison; sometimes they are totally uncoordinated and move to different drums. But they are faithful to do their own things as the warmth of the sun hits their solar batteries.

> **Psalm 149:3**
> *Let them praise his name in the dance: let them sing praises unto him with the timbrel and harp.*

These two little artificial beauties need nothing but sunshine, and they are content as long as their batteries get recharged. But they have another friend who has given up the ghost. No matter how much sun Pinkie gets, she won't budge. She stands there, not even trying to go through the motions of the sunshine dance, as if it's beneath her dignity to participate. And the whole problem is her battery needs to be replaced.

> **Ezekiel 18:30**
> *Therefore I will judge you, O house of Israel, every one according to his ways, saith the Lord God. Repent, and turn yourselves from all your transgressions; so iniquity shall not be your ruin.*

Their orchestrated antics remind me of people in church. Some people are more than willing to participate, even though they don't always blend in with the congregation. They willingly lift their hands in praise to worship our Lord, and they lift their voices in praise—even if their singing is more of a joyful noise than a beautiful melody. And then there are those who go through the motions of worship, but all it is is an act of trying to blend in rather than true worship.

> **Isaiah 29:13**
> *Wherefore the Lord said, Forasmuch as this people draw near me with their mouth, and with their lips do honour me, but have removed their heart far from me, and their fear toward me is taught by the precept of men.*

Undoubtedly, there are people like that in all kinds of places. They show up and want to do right, and they do blend in. Sometimes, however, they lack joy. These are the ones who are there in their bodies, but their hearts have not made the connection with the Lord. These are the ones who serve Him under a sense of obligation and may even be afraid of offending Him because of their perceived imperfection.

These people have not let their knowledge of the Lord go from their heads to their hearts—a journey of about 18 inches. Because their souls have not gone through a spiritual rebirth, they don't respond with an attitude that brings them pleasure. They seem to be caught up in what pleases other people more than what would please God.

> **Romans 12:2**
> *And be not conformed to this world: but be ye transformed by the renewing of your mind, that ye may prove what is that good, and acceptable, and perfect, will of God.*

So, praise-ers have an inside track to the heart of our Father. They are like Scarlett and Vi dancing in the sunshine. And those who are like Pinkie might need to get their spiritual battery checked. After all, there won't be any Energizer batteries in Heaven, and our time to get right with the Father is today—for today is the day of salvation.

2 Corinthians 6:2
For he saith, I have heard thee in a time accepted, and in the day of salvation have I succored thee: behold, now is the accepted time; behold, now is the day of salvation.

A CHRISTMAS LOVE LETTER
(Discerning God's Word)

When I was a child, I really, really, REALLY wanted a certain doll for Christmas. Now, sixty-something years later, I can't even remember her name, but this baby could crawl and cry, and I think she was even able to wet her pants. After I wrote my letter to make my request known to Santa, I was confident that he would fulfill my wish. As Christmas grew closer, I could almost feel the joy of holding my new baby.

On Christmas Eve, my parents took the family on a ride to look at Christmas lights while "Santa" made his delivery to our house. I just knew that my baby would be waiting when we returned home.

After our ride around town, we opened our packages, and I did indeed have one, but when I opened it, the gift was not what I expected. Instead of my requested doll, I got something totally unexpected... a letter to me from Santa.

Wow! Although I was let down, I was elated that Santa took the time to write me a real letter! The very fact that he noticed my wants thrilled me to no end—but where was my baby?

As I read his letter, I found out that he was not able to find that baby anywhere that year, and he promised he would do his best to get it for me next year. He was definitely aware of my wants, and he would be on the lookout for it. It was up to me just to be patient and keep being good because he cared about me and my wants.

As I grew older, I realized that my mom had penned the letter, and when the next year came, I did indeed have my special little one. But even though I had not received my dolly when I had first asked for it, it did arrive, and I was doubly blessed… to have gotten a personal letter from Santa one year and, eventually, the next year, my coveted doll.

Now, as an adult, I realize there are letters that are much more important than a letter from Santa, and gifts that will never grow old or disappear over time, as my baby doll did. The letters are letters written by scribes over earlier centuries who gave mankind messages from the Lord of the Universe to create the Bible. And the greatest gift is God's Son, Jesus—not to mention all the other gifts, benefits, and promises He gives us by being His children.

When we read the Bible, we learn of God's love for us in so many ways. The Word says:

> **John 3:16**
> *For God so loved the world that He GAVE His only begotten Son, that whosoever believeth in Him should not perish, but have everlasting life.*

That would be the greatest gift. But there is more—much more.

As His child, He loads us down with gifts—benefits—too:

> **Psalm 103:1**
> *Bless the Lord, O my soul: and all that is within me, bless his holy name. Bless the Lord, O my soul, and forget not all his benefits:*

The Word tells us some gifts are better than others.

> **1 Corinthians 12:31**
> *But covet earnestly the best gifts.*

He speaks of spiritual gifts, but He knows we as humans give gifts too. And He has promised to give good gifts to us as well.

Matthew 7:11
If ye then, being evil, know how to give good gifts unto your children, how much more shall your Father which is in heaven give good things to them that ask him?

    I've been told over the years since I became a Christian that the Bible is God's love letter to us, and it is full of His promises. But unlike the letter I got from my imaginary Santa, the promises of the Bible are true. On the other hand, like my make-believe letter, good things come to those who wait.

    Are you trusting in His promises that He made in His Word? If you are, you may have to be faithful to wait—but you will never be disappointed.

BUT GOD...
(God's Mercy and Grace)

There have been times in my life when everything seemed to be cattywampus. No matter what I did or how hard I tried to correct the situation, it just got worse and worse. I was on the verge of despair, wanting to give up. But God...

I was in a bad marriage with four little ones and a husband who didn't want the responsibility. Life was difficult, to say the least. Finding a way to take care of my babies while I found a paying job... getting my oldest to kindergarten and the others to sitters... putting food on the table and a roof over our heads... having transportation and juggling five jobs at one time. I could have easily given up, but God...

When I graduated from high school in 1969, I was proud to have received a number of scholarships for furthering my education. However, my spouse (the deadbeat dad) would not allow me to go to secondary college. I stayed home and had baby after baby and felt like I had let my benefactors down because I didn't honor their faith in me. After 17 years—long after that marriage ended—I finally did go finish my schooling and found a job as a teacher. I can proudly say that I started teaching when I was 41 and taught for 24 years, retiring at age 65. And it would not have happened, but God...

One of my dreams as a young wife (in my second marriage) was to be able to visit Israel. An organization I was active in, Women's Aglow, was sponsoring a trip to the Holy Land, and I had put in my reservation. Just before the final payment was due, I found out that I needed a few hundred more dollars, so I had to let go of that dream. Many years later, when I was teaching language arts in junior high, Holocaust survivor Helen Colin recommended that she and the other survivors in Houston sponsor me on a teacher's trip to Poland and Israel to study the Holocaust. Although it had been delayed by 20 years or more, I finally had my dream fulfilled. I could have given up, but God…

My beautiful mother was a vibrant, healthy sixty-nine-year-old who walked two miles a day. When she had a stroke in her bedroom in March 1992, her world came crashing down. It left her with her left side paralyzed and unable to complete even the simplest tasks for herself. She was a determined lady who found her identity in baking, so she found a way to resume her passion, albeit with the help of a bread machine. Even with her physical disability, she lived a full, vibrant life until the age of 91. She could have easily given up and stopped trying, but God…

My second husband ended up being a dialysis patient. He went through almost five years of treatment. He and I both were discouraged at various times while he underwent his medical care. There were at least three times when I was on my teaching job in Bay City and he was in the dialysis center in Wharton where he had a crisis. I had to return home quickly to take him to an ER in Sugarland. It was overwhelming to not know what was going to happen each day, but God…

Think of the "but God…" experiences you have had. You could have been killed, but God protected you. You could have died from an illness, but God helped you get well. You had a challenge that was bigger than anything you could ever imagine, but God gave you the strength to endure. You had a dream that seemed to be shattered, but God restored your hope and gave you a new beginning.

So, look up, my friend, and realize where you might be if there had not been a "but God…" experience in your life.

Matthew 21:22
And all things, whatsoever ye shall ask in prayer, believing, ye shall receive.

Romans 10:17
So then faith cometh by hearing, and hearing by the word of God.

Mark 11:22-24
And Jesus answering saith unto them, Have faith in God. For verily I say unto you, That whosoever shall say unto this mountain, Be thou removed, and be thou cast into the sea; and shall not doubt in his heart, but shall believe that those things which he saith shall come to pass; he shall have whatsoever he saith.
Therefore I say unto you, What things soever ye desire, when ye pray, believe that ye receive them, and ye shall have them.

1 Corinthians 2:5
That your faith should not stand in the wisdom of men, but in the power of God.

Jeremiah 29:11
For I know the thoughts that I think toward you, saith the Lord, thoughts of peace, and not of evil, to give you an expected end.

Romans 8:28
And we know that all things work together for good to them that love God, to them who are the called according to his purpose.

THE ROSE THAT DIDN'T DIE
(Truthfulness)

In 2022, the Wharton Lion's Club presented a rose to me in honor of my brother, Leroy Dettling, who passed away the previous December. I was so proud of that beautiful flower! I protected it from getting crushed as I drove home, and as soon as I got to my house, I made sure to put it in a vase with water. I was going to keep that white rose alive as long as I possibly could.

The next morning, I checked my prize again, and it didn't look any less beautiful than it had the day before. Because it was so perfect, I studied it very carefully. What a shock I received when I found out that the flower I had protected so faithfully turned out to be plastic! I could have drowned it in water or never watered it at all, and the outcome would have been the same—still pretty, still plastic, still fake.

How like other things that come to us in life? Things advertised on TV; products that are new and improved; vehicles that are top of the line; foods that are indescribably delicious; insurance that covers every problem that you could possibly imagine; legal services that will recoup all the losses someone has endured due to someone else's negligence; medications that will heal what ails you (if you live past the list of warnings they give); friendships that turn out to be solely for another person's gain; investments that will bring you great wealth; diets and weight loss schemes that will transform your body in just a matter of days—and the list goes on and on.

I've heard that the way to tell a counterfeit is to study the genuine article. If you know what to look for in something that is real, you recognize the fake when it comes across your path. So the main idea is not to major on the imitations, but to be so familiar with the real thing that the fake will stand out like a neon light.

This condition seeps into more than just day-to-day living. The Bible warns us that there will be shysters in the last days... people who want us to believe lies concerning God Himself. It goes so far as to say there will be wolves in sheep's clothing. It also compares the day-to-day actions of people to good fruit and bad fruit.

Before you are fooled by the imposters, be sure to be able to recognize the real deal. Your life—especially your spiritual life—may depend on it.

Matthew 7:15
Beware of false prophets, which come to you in sheep's clothing, but inwardly they are ravening wolves.

Luke 6:43
For a good tree bringeth not forth corrupt fruit; neither doth a corrupt tree bring forth good fruit.

Matthew 24:24
For there shall arise false Christs, and false prophets, and shall shew great signs and wonders; insomuch that, if it were possible, they shall deceive the very elect.

DO YOU SEE ME?
(our identity in Christ)

Someone recently asked me, "Do you see me?"

The answer was obvious because I did see him, but then he asked, "Do you really SEE me?"

He went on to say, "Do you see what's inside of me—my hopes, my dreams, my fears, my insecurities, my abilities?"

Whoa! That was a loaded question, and I began to think of all the ways a person longs to be seen.

When I pass someone selling something outside of a store and I am not in the market to buy, I intentionally don't "see" him or her. It's the same look people give me when they don't want to hear my spiel about looking at my books. I realize not everyone is a potential customer, so I don't take the rejection personally.

But there are times when not "seeing" someone shows a lack of compassion or insight.

It's easy to think that because someone is homeless, they are homeless by choice. But taking the time to interact with them helps to understand their predicament. Maybe it was caused by a financial disaster—like job loss, divorce, bankruptcy, or health problems.

> **James 2:8–9**
> If you really keep the royal law found in Scripture, *"Love your neighbor as yourself,"* you are doing right. But if you show favoritism, you sin and are convicted by the law as lawbreakers.

Sometimes it is caused by our own attitudes of being better than someone else. It may be that we are more educated than another person and we let that become a deciding factor in our relationships. Or it could be snobbery in reverse—thinking that because we are not as educated or financially well off, we have nothing in common with another class of people. As children of God, we can't be held captive to the thought that God should "bless our four and no more."

Romans 2:11
For there is no respect of persons with God.

Think of the examples of people in the Bible who were not "seen" as God saw them. One of the top examples is David, who became the King of Israel. When the prophet Samuel came to anoint him to be the second King of Israel, his dad Jesse was reluctant to tell Samuel that he had another son. That's when he was reminded that God does not look on outward appearance.

1 Samuel 16:7
People look at the outward appearance, but the Lord looks at the heart.

Think back to the story of Joseph, the much-loved son of Jacob. He was a dreamer who trusted God, even though his brothers sold him into slavery. What if you had seen him working as a servant in Potiphar's house? Worse yet, if you dealt with him as a prisoner in Pharaoh's prison? Would you have recognized him as someone God had chosen for the important purpose of saving a nation? But God used him in spite of the horrid circumstances.

Genesis 45:7–8
But God sent me ahead of you to preserve for you a remnant on earth and to save your lives by a great deliverance. So then, it was not you who sent me here, but God.

If you can learn how to see people—and really SEE them—you have an insight into the heart of God. And if you think the real you is not being seen, then you need to rethink thoughts about yourself and start seeing yourself as God sees you. He does care, and He has chosen you for whatever task He has assigned you, whether you are rich or poor or educated or not. Trust Him.

Jeremiah 29:11
For I know the plans I have for you," declares the Lord, "plans to prosper you and not to harm you, plans to give you hope and a future.

FEAR NOT
(Being brave)

Fear has a hold on many people in many ways. I am one of those people who didn't know anything I was really afraid of. Spiders, snakes, scorpions, other critters—were just a few of the things on my "I'm not scared of anything!" list. However, I had my comeuppance one winter in Colorado when I had the experience of being terrified—and it was not because of a critter, but it was from nature itself.

My husband and I were taking a ride through the Colorado National Monument Park, and I expected just to see beautiful scenery. The scenes were absolutely breathtaking to begin with. Then they transformed into more than just breathtaking—they became downright intimidating. Humongous rock formations, snowcapped mountain tops, valleys that seemed to have no bottom, rock walls standing like sentries guarding their precious kingdom.

Psalm 56:11
In God have I put my trust: I will not be afraid what man (or cliffs) can do unto me.

As we followed the paved roadway, we entered into some of the most exquisite land formations on God's green earth. We ascended higher and higher, and the drive became more and more unnerving. The road, which was well-maintained, was missing something: side rails. Just 15 inches from the side of the road, for many miles along the journey, someone could easily drop into oblivion—and it would not be easy to rescue them. And I DID NOT want to be that person!!!

Psalm 3:6
I will not be afraid of ten thousands of people (or rock formations), that have set themselves against me round about.

Every round went higher and higher, like Jacob's ladder. I breathed easy every time we found a section with a rail, but it seemed the rail-less sections were far more prevalent than the rails.

Joshua 1:9
Have not I commanded thee? Be strong and of a good courage; be not afraid, neither be thou dismayed: for the Lord thy God is with thee whithersoever thou goest.

Holding my breath did no good—and neither did closing my eyes to the potential threat. Sucking in my breath with every intimidation was useless in overcoming my concern.

2 Timothy 1:7
For God hath not given us the spirit of fear; but of power, and of love, and of a sound mind.

My fear was irrational. After all, thousands of tourists had ridden over these roads, and to my knowledge, no one had fallen off the cliff. But by trusting in the Lord and in my husband's driving skill, I completed the challenge—and meekly, I had to admit that I'm not as invincible as I'd like to think I am.

I've known all the scriptures about fear for as long as I've been a Christian. This little journey was a hands-on reminder that I serve a God who is a great deliverer. No matter what causes me to shake in my shoes, He will carry me through.

WHAT TOOL ARE YOU?

A few weeks ago, when we were driving home from a trip we had taken, my husband asked me a strange question.

Without any explanation, he asked me, "If you were a tool, what kind of tool would you be?"

It took me only a minute to respond. "I would be a funnel."

"A funnel? Why a funnel? I would have never thought of that."

I began my explanation so he could easily understand my reasoning.

"A funnel is used to fill other containers. I want to help fill others with faith in God and in His goodness."

Then I got to thinking about other tools and other ways they are used... hammers, screwdrivers, sandpaper, chopping hoes, shovels, wrenches, pliers, levels, extension cords, flashlights, drills.

Right off the top of my head, I knew what I would NOT want to be... a hammer, a screwdriver, a chopping hoe, or a shovel. Those items seem to me to be self-explanatory—they could cause damage to fragile souls. But then my husband gave me a few more ideas for tools that might be helpful for the Kingdom: wrenches, levels, extension cords, flashlights. That's when I had to have him explain the reasons behind some of these choices.

A wrench? Sometimes people need an adjustment in the way they think.

A level? To keep others from going off the deep end from feeling inadequate—or to keep them from getting so full of themselves that their heads are in the clouds.

An extension cord? To help people plug in to the life they

could have in God.

A flashlight? Actually, that one comes from the scripture that says, "Thy Word is a lamp unto my feet and a light unto my path."

Wow! All kinds of tools for all kinds of situations! Then I tweaked the idea and wondered about kitchen tools and what would I be in that scenario?

Once more, I would want to be gentle and encouraging... maybe a spatula or a spoon or a whisk. But the kitchen has tools that could be harsh as well: potato masher, meat cleaver, steak knives, cheese shredder, egg beater.

If a kitchen or workroom has dozens of tools with dozens of uses, then we as children of God should be open to the variety of ways that He can use us as tools for His Kingdom.

What tool are you?

1 Corinthians 12:28
And God hath set some in the church, first apostles, secondarily prophets, thirdly teachers, after that miracles, then gifts of healings, helps, governments, diversities of tongues.

Titus 2:15
These things speak, and exhort, and rebuke with all authority. Let no man despise thee.

Revelation 3:19
As many as I love, I rebuke and chasten: be zealous therefore, and repent.

1 Thessalonians 5:11
Wherefore comfort yourselves together, and edify one another, even as also ye do.

DISPLACED FAITH
(Overcoming Failure)

One cool morning in January, I plugged in a small electric heater to take the chill out of the room. I could almost feel the warmth as I turned on the switch. However, I was greatly disappointed when no hot air came forth. I found out that my faith in that electric outlet was useless, and it made me wonder how many things people have faith in, only to realize their faith is not in something that will supply the need.

> **James 2:26**
> *For as the body without the spirit is dead, so faith without works is dead also.*

How often have you turned on a light switch just to have it make a big flash as it burned out? Or, like me, you used an outlet that produced no power? Maybe you've tried to start a car only to get a whir-whir-whir sound and no combustion. Maybe you have bought something from a store and had great expectation for it, only to find that you seemingly threw your money down the drain.

What's even worse is when you place your confidence in a person or a group, and the things you thought they could do turn into failed expectations. That happens over and over again in stores, restaurants, and places of public service.

> **Romans 3:4**
> *God forbid: yea, let God be true, but every man a liar.*

I've found there is only one Person who hasn't let me down. Even on my worst days, He has had my back. There have been times that I have had to be patient and wait on His answer, but He delivered.

> **Mark 11:22**
> *And Jesus answering saith unto them, Have faith in God.*

I've gone to Him with all kinds of problems: financial, emotional, physical—even relationships—and He has shown me the way to deal with these things that happen in life.

So, I've come to the conclusion that as long as men's feet are made of clay, it's very possible—and even probable—that they will let me down.

> **2 Thessalonians 3:2**
> *And that we may be delivered from unreasonable and wicked men: for all men have not faith.*

SELF-MADE MAN? NOT LIKELY!
(community)

Way back in 1623, an author named John Donne proclaimed, "No man is an island." All kinds of people got on that bandwagon in the 1960s, and we all professed our need for each other. One of the ways we shared that message was through a song by that name, "No Man Is an Island," by Joan Baez, and people were singing or humming along.

There is a new mantra today: we are better together. I've heard it in church, in public meetings, and when friends gather. I, for one, believe it is true.

Over and over again, the Bible admonishes people to gather together. In fact, there are 61 references to people coming together for a common purpose.

> **Luke 8:4**
> *And when much people were gathered together, and were come to him out of every city, he spake by a parable...*

It amuses me when people call themselves self-made. After all, did they weave and sew the clothes they wear? How about their shoes? Did they raise and kill the animal that provided the leather, or raise the material their shoes are made of? Do they have any jewelry that came from a refiner or artisan, or do they drive a vehicle that is made of metal or uses gasoline? If they have anything that falls in any of these categories, the person is not legitimately self-made.

Let's take that idea a step further. We can't go to a grocery store without buying something that someone else has grown or manufactured—food, cleaning supplies, vegetables, coffee. We can't even go to a store unless we travel on a road that someone else created and paved, and ride in a vehicle manufactured by someone else. Where is the autonomy in that?

I admit that there are some people who seem to be self-sufficient, but even at that, their success depends on the foundation that someone else may have laid—whether it be creating electricity, or a computer and program, paper, pen, ink, anything that is not in its raw state. Those folks who live alone and relish their solidarity are few and far between. The rest of us are a part of the herd mentality.

My idea of a self-made man may be extreme. Maybe holding a person accountable to anyone and everyone who had a part in providing food, shelter, and clothing is not a fair way to gauge autonomy, but it emphasizes humanity's need of one person for others. The one person the Bible talks about who seemed to be totally autonomous was the cousin of Jesus, John the Baptist.

He probably lived in a cave, too, without sheets or bedding, and certainly without the comforts of home. He could have killed the camel that he used for his clothing. With a diet of locusts and wild honey, no one in the marketplace could take responsibility for providing his food, and no one paved the roads that he walked down. After he left the home of his parents, Zacharias and Elizabeth, he was totally on his own.

> **Matthew 3:4**
> *And the same John had his raiment of camel's hair, and a leathern girdle about his loins; and his meat was locusts and wild honey.*

Even Adam and Eve were not self-sufficient. After all, God killed the animals that He used to cover their nakedness. Their children depended on each other as well.

So the next time someone professes to be self-made and extols their own abilities, take it with a grain of salt. Judgment Day is coming.

Luke 12:20-21
But God said unto him, Thou fool, this night thy soul shall be required of thee: then whose shall those things be, which thou hast provided? So is he that layeth up treasure for himself, and is not rich toward God.

Romans 12:3
For I say, through the grace given unto me, to every man that is among you, not to think of himself more highly than he ought to think; but to think soberly, according as God hath dealt to every man the measure of faith.

1 Corinthians 4:7
For who maketh thee to differ from another? and what hast thou that thou didst not receive? now if thou didst receive it, why dost thou glory, as if thou hadst not received it?

THE FAVOR OF GOD
(Blessings)

People tend to pray for a lot of things, but I saw faith in action one day when my husband and I were playing a round of Yahtzee. He prayed, asking God for favor and to grant him some 2's because he needed to get 2's on his score card. I giggled incessantly as he made his request known, but that didn't stop him from praying. He went boldly to the Throne of God like David did. He told God that if he found favor in His sight, would He please let him roll some 2's?

Now that kind of praying may sound frivolous, but we were reminded that God does care about the little things in our lives—even in a game of Yahtzee. We saw God in action, and we were in awe at the speed in which He answered.

Because we believe God hears us when we pray, it wasn't unusual for my husband to pray about getting some deuces.

> **1 John 5:15**
> "...we know that he heareth us whatsoever we ask, we know that we have the petitions which we have asked of him."

The more he prayed, the more I giggled. He told the Lord that if He gave him the 2's, he would give Him the glory—and that is exactly what happened. He put the dice in the cup and immediately rolled three 2's. Now, three 2's may not seem to be a big thing, but after praying, it was pretty impressive! But what happened next was even more impressive. The second roll landed another 2. Could it be that one more 2 was possible?

Imagine our joy when that was exactly what happened...

another 2, giving my man a Yahtzee in 2's! We laughed... we shouted... we praised God... we rejoiced!

I was reminded of:

> **Proverbs 12:2**
> *"A good man shall obtain favor of Jehovah."*

It would have been easy to explain it away as a fluke, but we both knew better. It wasn't because of the 2's on the dice, but because of the realization that our Lord hears the prayers of His children.

> **In Exodus 33:17,**
> *The Lord said to Moses, "I will do this thing also that you have requested, for you have found favor in my sight, and I know you by name."*

He gave my husband reassurance that he had found favor in His sight. It was a glorious event, and we both were thankful to have witnessed His goodness.

My husband and I realize that life has a tendency to move very fast, and sometimes we wonder if the decisions we make are pleasing to Him—but He gave us reassurance that we do have His favor, and there is absolutely nothing better than that!

After that episode, I got to thinking about how many times God has shown favor to us without us even realizing it. Think of the times you have had a close call on the highway. I can remember times when I had such a close call that I could almost feel angel wings between me and a passing car!

Even Queen Esther in the Old Testament asked for favor when she was petitioning King Ahasuerus. Although God is not mentioned by name, He is still very much in the story. Why else would she have asked her handmaids to fast with her before she went in to the king?

We have a Heavenly Father, and we can trust Him to take

care of us at all times. That is the true favor of God. Put Him to the test—you'll be glad you did.

Philippians 4:6
In nothing be anxious; but in everything by prayer and supplication with thanksgiving let your requests be made known unto God.

1 Peter 4:8
For the eyes of the Lord are over the righteous, and his ears are open unto their prayers: but the face of the Lord is against them that do evil.

Proverbs 15:29
The Lord is far from the wicked: but he heareth the prayer of the righteous.

DEBUNKING OLD WIVES TALES AND OTHER MISCONCEPTIONS
(Wisdom/Knowledge)

When I was a child, my mother used to tell me all kinds of stuff that sounded educated, and I trusted her, so as far as I knew, it was truth. However, as I've grown older, I've found that many of the things that she said were true because of her experiences were not necessarily true in everyone's life. Because of that, I have had to adjust my thinking.

The stories were not earth-shattering, but in my childish mind, I believed that if my momma said it, then it was undoubtedly true.

> **John 8:32**
> *And ye shall know the truth, and the truth shall make you free.*

One of the things she said was kind of a teasing thing. Sometimes, when toast got burnt, she had a ploy to get us/me to eat it anyway.

"Eating burnt toast is good for you," she said. "It will make you pretty."

Potato peels were just as beneficial... they were another one of nature's remedies to help make us pretty.

> **1 Timothy 4:7**
> *But refuse profane and old wives' fables.*

I still eat burnt toast occasionally and peels from a baked or boiled potato. Whether it improved my looks or not, I'll let you be the judge. But I have acquired a taste especially for the outer parts of a baked potato and even steal them from my husband's plate when we eat out.

I know there had to be other situations, but the one that convinced me that Mom didn't always know what she was talking about was when my husband and I moved to Colorado and I became somewhat familiar with snow.

Really low-hanging, wet clouds when the temperature was in the mid-30s caused Mom to predict snowfall.

"Those clouds have snow in them," she said, and occasionally, she was right.

But when I was in Grand Junction, Colorado, I learned snowfall does not always depend on a certain look in the clouds or even a temperature in the 30s. I've seen it snow with the sun shining or the clouds so far up in the sky that I never knew it was snowing unless I was in it or looking out a window. I've seen snow in the teens and twenties and 40s. Once, I saw snow falling when there was a thunderstorm going on. Those happenings shot Mom's theories all to pieces!

> **2 Timothy 2:15**
> *Study to shew thyself approved unto God, a workman that needeth not to be ashamed, rightly dividing the word of truth.*

And now, as an adult, I find many situations that may not always tell the whole truth. Product advertisers are prime examples.

Listening to or reading ads that may, in fact, help the problem but in the long run may add to a person's health crisis is one example. By the time the ad finishes the disclaimer, it's a wonder anyone is still alive after taking the supposed cure.

Political ads are another source of half-truths. These advertisers know if they told you the whole truth that they might lose you as a potential voter.

So what is a person to believe? Test the spirit and see if there is truth in what is being said. Don't automatically accept what someone else is telling you, even if you have high regard for that person. Above all, ask God for discernment to know the truth, and indeed, the truth shall set you free.

Philippians 4:8
Finally, brethren, whatsoever things are true, whatsoever things are honest, whatsoever things are just, whatsoever things are pure, whatsoever things are lovely, whatsoever things are of good report; if there be any virtue, and if there be any praise, think on these things.

Romans 3:4
...By no means! Let God be true, though every one were a liar.

THEY ARE WITH US STILL
(Relationships)

From as long as anyone can remember, people have wondered about life after the grave. Some people seem to be obsessed with it, while others accept the fact of a beloved friend's passing, and some may marvel when they receive something that seems like a visit from beyond the grave.

When someone dies, friends and family offer comforting words like, "That person will always be with you as long as you have the memories."

> **Philippians 1:3**
> *I thank my God upon every remembrance of you.*

I used to think that was a platitude, but then I saw the reality of the statement as I thought of some different ways the dead still speak.

When I was cleaning a storeroom at my house, I found packets of letters and cards with special messages, addressed to me. Each one of those was a visitation from beyond the grave. There were birthday cards, anniversary cards, little notes written on scraps of paper. There was nothing eerie or supernatural about it at all, but they were filled with love.

> **John 14:26**
> *But the Comforter, which is the Holy Ghost, whom the Father will send in my name, he shall teach you all things, and bring all things to your remembrance, whatsoever I have said unto you.*

My daughter loves to make strudel because my mom taught her how. She makes tortillas because her other grandma taught. As simple as they are, every time my daughter makes strudel or tortillas, or does anything like her grandmas did, she is having a visitation from beyond the grave.

Anytime a person does something that someone else taught them, then the memory of that loved one is visiting whoever they left on earth. Like the way someone folds clothes, or cooks a pot roast, or plays a game, or tells a story. Memories are the things that the past is made of. Most are understandable, but some touch heartstrings more than others. My husband had that situation recently as he was cleaning out his desk.

His previous wife knew she was dying from cancer. In the time that she had on earth, she tucked messages away for him in places where she knew he would find them. As he was cleaning out his desk, he found one of her notes carefully tucked away for him to find. It was a melancholy moment for him, sparked by contact with a loved one from the past.

2 Timothy 1:3
I thank God, whom I serve from my forefathers with pure conscience, that without ceasing I have remembrance of thee in my prayers night and day.

Life is made of relationships with people who have crossed our paths, whether it be previous mates, parents, or grandparents.

Hebrews 12:1
Wherefore seeing we also are compassed about with so great a cloud of witnesses, let us lay aside every weight, and the sin which doth so easily beset us, and let us run with patience the race that is set before us.

After all is said and done, the greatest gift from beyond the grave is the gift that Jesus gave us before His cruel death on Calvary—the way He instituted what we now call Communion, or the Lord's Supper. This sacrament is simple enough to be carried on anywhere throughout the world, yet profound enough to make an impact. Although Jesus did die, His death was not the end of His life. Thank God for His resurrection, and thank God for every remembrance of Him.

1 Corinthians 11:24
And when he had given thanks, he brake it, and said, Take, eat: this is my body, which is broken for you: this do in remembrance of me.

THE JOY OF LITTLE VICTORIES
(Endurance/Perseverance)

All of us have them at one time or another, but not all of us recognize them. Little victories are things that may not be big and grand, but necessary reminders of accomplishment nonetheless.

Exactly what is a "little victory"? It's one of those things on your to-do list that got done, even if nothing else did. It's something that reminds you that you are NOT a failure, even when nothing else was completed. It is, to put it bluntly, a victory.

Sometimes it seems that I complete all that I want to and then some, but there are other times when I do good to accomplish anything at all! When that happens, I remember to claim little victories.

There was a time when I had a room to clean that was full to the brim with junk that had been collected over many years. I tried my best to make progress, but the odds were against me. No sooner would I fill a trash bag or a giveaway box than another situation took priority over my cleaning. After hours of seemingly making no progress, I realized I did indeed have little victories to celebrate—1 giveaway box filled, 2 trash bags to toss, and 1 bed found under the clutter for sleeping. Four little victories, in fact!

Another time I had about a half dozen bills to pay, several cards to write, grocery shopping to do, a floor that needed to be vacuumed, another floor to be mopped, and a bathroom to be cleaned. By the time I got done, about all that I really had to show for my day was a scrubbed toilet, a few groceries bought, and a vacuumed floor. Not much in the eyes of the world, but little victories nonetheless.

Then there are the little victories that happen when something we have needed FINALLY gets taken care of—like finding something that was lost. Several years ago, I was in my garage, getting rid of trash. When I got to the bottom of one of my boxes, something with a reddish-brown color caught my eye. As I emptied the box to get to the object, lo and behold, I found one of my post office keys, one that had been MIA for years! It had been missing for so long that I had given up the hunt a long time ago. And yet, when I found it, I counted it as a big little victory.

Little victories remind me that I actually DID accomplish something—I was not just spinning my wheels. Those are the kinds of things that keep me going.

In the history of the world, there have been major battles and minor skirmishes. The little victories along the way helped the troops to keep up their morale, eventually winning the war.

Celebrate little victories!

> **Zechariah 4:10**
> *For who hath despised the day of small things? for they shall rejoice, and shall see the plummet in the hand of Zerubbabel.*
>
> **Isaiah 28:10**
> *For precept must be upon precept, precept upon precept; line upon line, line upon line; here a little, and there a little.*

Find your little victories in everything you do.

Ecclesiastes 3
To everything there is a season,
and a time to every purpose under the heaven:
a time to be born, and a time to die;
a time to plant, and a time to pluck up that which
is planted;
a time to kill, and a time to heal;
a time to break down, and a time to build up;
a time to weep, and a time to laugh;
a time to mourn, and a time to dance;
a time to cast away stones,
and a time to gather stones together;
a time to embrace, and a time to refrain from embracing;
a time to get, and a time to lose;
a time to keep, and a time to cast away;
a time to rend, and a time to sew;
a time to keep silence, and a time to speak;
a time to love, and a time to hate;
a time of war, and a time of peace.

ALL PARTS WORK TOGETHER
(The Body of Christ)

When I was a child, I was fascinated with my thumb. I sucked it almost constantly for comfort from the imagined problems in my life. At least until I was 5. That was when my dad threatened to make me sleep with the chickens if I didn't stop. Needless to say, I had a few teary nights, but I stopped. His ploy worked!

As I grew older, my thumb wasn't nearly as important. It got to where I didn't even pay it much mind unless I had a cut from peeling vegetables or a hangnail. Other than that, my thumb didn't serve a very important purpose in my life. I just accepted it as it was, and life went on.

But one week in the past, something happened. I don't know how, but somehow, someway, I sprained it and found out just how important that two-and-a-half-inch digit is, and I missed it greatly as a fully functioning part of my body.

Every move I made had my body screaming out—not just my thumb, but my other fingers, my wrist, my arm, the rest of my hand. My other hand reached out to caress the suffering part of my body. I tried to plan my movements so that my poor little thumb would not have to endure any more pain.

Realizing how important my thumb is gave me new insight to **1 Corinthians 12**, where it talks about the members of the Body of Christ needing each other.

> *Yes, the body has many parts, not just one part.*
> *If the foot says, "I am not a part of the body because I am not a hand," that does not make it any less a part of the body.*

And what would you think if you heard an ear say, "I am not part of the body because I am only an ear and not an eye"? Would that make it any less a part of the body? Suppose the whole body were an eye—then how would you hear? Or if your whole body were just one big ear, how could you smell anything?
But that isn't the way God has made us. He has made many parts for our bodies and has put each part just where he wants it.
What a strange thing a body would be if it had only one part!
So he has made many parts, but still there is only one body.
The eye can never say to the hand, "I don't need you." The head can't say to the feet, "I don't need you." (Living Bible)

Pain in my thumb and that verse have helped me to realize an important spiritual truth… Denomination does not matter… God needs all of us to accomplish His purposes, and we are all part of His Body.

He has a plan for the Baptists, as He does for the Methodists and the Pentecostals. His plan also includes Presbyterians, Lutherans, Episcopalians, Catholics, and non-denominationals. And don't forget… the Amish, Mennonites, Messianic Jews, and all others that profess Jesus as Lord. Although we are many, we are one, and He uses each of our groups as He pleases. We are all brothers and sisters because of the sacrifice Jesus made on our behalf.

If one part hurts, we all hurt, just like my thumb has my whole body feeling pain. Don't you dare look down on any other part of the Lord's Body because He has included it for His own divine purpose. We all truly are part of His body, and we do need one another. May His will be done in our lives.

John 17:21 (TLB)
My prayer for all of them is that they will be of one heart and mind, just as you and I are, Father—that just as you are in me and I am in you, so they will be in us, and the world will believe you sent me.

THE AUDACITY OF YOUTH
(Foolishness)

As I grow older, I look back over the years and see how pompous and arrogant I was as a youth and later on as a young mother.

When I was a teen, I could easily climb from the floor to the top of the kitchen counter so I could clean the top shelves of the cabinets. I could lay on my back and ride an invisible bicycle without blinking an eye. Getting on my hands and knees to mop the kitchen floor was a breeze—in fact, almost enjoyable.

I was told to enjoy those abilities while they lasted because I would not be able to do them all my life. I didn't pay much attention and kept on doing what I did.

Then, as a young mother, I prided myself on being able to carry a heavy load of laundry while I was pregnant or holding one of my babies. There seemed to be nothing that I couldn't tote from one place to another. Matriarchs warned me that I would regret those moves someday, but I acted like I was invincible.

But, when I hit my 40's, things started to change. I got an unpleasant surprise in a volleyball game at the junior high I taught at when the faculty played the students. As I tried to hit a return ball, my knee went one way, my leg the other, and I was in intense pain for days. That torn meniscus signaled the beginning of knee troubles for the next 15 years, till I finally had both knees replaced.

I'm not going to give you a litany of aches and pains that I've had since the big 4-0, but you probably get the message. Each chapter of life is for a season, and we are not the ones who determine how long our seasons will last.

So many of us know of friends and family who did not live out their potential of three score and ten, and we mourned their untimely passing. Those of us who remain need to be mindful that our days are numbered.

We would be wise to remember the words of The Teacher in Ecclesiastes: 12 - *Remember now thy Creator in the days of thy youth, while the evil days come not, nor the years draw nigh,*

Ecclesiastes 12:7
Then shall the dust return to the earth as it was: and the spirit shall return unto God who gave it.

Isaiah 40:30
Even youths shall faint and be weary, and young men shall fall exhausted.

Proverbs 20:29
The glory of young men is their strength, but the splendor of old men is their gray hair.

Psalm 25:7
Remember not the sins of my youth or my transgressions; according to your steadfast love remember me, for the sake of your goodness, O Lord!

POWER OF PERSISTENT PRAYER
(Prayer)

Once upon a time, I was held captive in a rocking chair, and I needed someone to deliver me. It's a really weird story, and most people would find it too embarrassing to share, but I'm willing to share in hopes that it might be helpful to someone else who might need deliverance at some point in time.

It was a cool Tuesday morning, before the heat of summer had begun. Randy, my husband, had gone to play golf in Giddings, ten miles away from our home. I decided I was going to sit on the front porch for a while and just enjoy God's beautiful creation. I placed my cellphone down on top of the porch rail, then proceeded to set myself down in the antique wooden rocker. No sooner had I sat in the chair when, all of a sudden, the bottom of the chair gave out, and the comfort I was seeking became a nightmare! I was trapped and could not extricate myself.

What a predicament I had gotten myself into! My phone was just a few inches out of reach, and I didn't have enough leverage to grab hold of the railing. I began praying for Randy to return from golf early, but that did not happen.

Meekly and weakly, I started calling for help.

"Help! Please help me!"

We had no next-door neighbors, so it was very unlikely that my pleas would draw any attention. I started to yell more loudly.

"HELP ME! PLEASE!!! I NEED HELP!!!!!"

I had gone up a couple of decibels in my yelling, even hoping that someone driving by on Highway 77 would hear my screams and come to my aid. After about 15 minutes of useless noise and watching dozens of vehicles pass by, I knew I had to ramp my voice up as much as possible. So, I started blasting my request as loud as I possibly could. I aimed my voice to the west of our house, hoping the guys at the oilfield company across the road from us would be my rescuers.

"HELP! PLEASE HELP! I'M TRAPPED AND I CAN'T GET LOOSE! PLEASE, PLEASE, PLEASE COME HELP ME!"

By now, I had no pride left, and I screamed continuously at the top of my lungs for at least 30 minutes. Finally, someone came running from across the road, while the owner of the business came up our driveway in his pickup truck. They were both amazed that they even heard me at all! The two angels in oilfield garb could not believe what they saw — a white-haired older lady who was stuck like a cork in the bottom of a rickety old rocker.

With the men on each side of me, they grabbed my arms and pulled to get me loose. Within minutes of their arrival, I was finally free!

My backside was sore, but it wasn't damaged nearly as much as my pride. After Randy got home — an hour after I was set free — I ended up in ER just to make sure nothing was seriously injured, and it took several days to return to what previously was normal. And now that some time has gone by, I can see a spiritual message in this crazy happenstance.

Time and time again, the Bible talks about the virtue of persistence. If I had not been persistent, I would not have gotten the help I needed to be set free. I could have not-so-easily suffered in my precarious position until my husband arrived, but I was ready to throw my pride out the window just to get some much-needed relief.

So often in life, we pray for answers to problems, and when answers don't come like we think they should, we are likely to give up just before a breakthrough. But when that happens, think about the gold miner who was panning for gold. After months went by, he never did strike it big. Out of frustration, he sold his claim, and the new owner struck it rich in just a few days' time.

So, my friend, be vigilant. Your answer may be just around the corner.

Matthew 7:7–8
Ask, and it shall be given you; seek, and ye shall find; knock, and it shall be opened unto you:
For every one that asketh receiveth; and he that seeketh findeth; and to him that knocketh it shall be opened.

Luke 11:9–10
And I say unto you, Ask, and it shall be given you; seek, and ye shall find; knock, and it shall be opened unto you.
For every one that asketh receiveth; and he that seeketh findeth; and to him that knocketh it shall be opened.

Luke 18:5–7
Yet because this widow troubleth me, I will avenge her, lest by her continual coming she weary me.
And the Lord said, Hear what the unjust judge saith.
And shall not God avenge his own elect, which cry day and night unto him, though he bear long with them?

Luke 11:6–8
For a friend of mine in his journey is come to me, and I have nothing to set before him?
And he from within shall answer and say, Trouble me not: the door is now shut, and my children are with me in bed; I cannot rise and give thee.
I say unto you, though he will not rise and give him, because he is his friend, yet because of his importunity, he will rise and give him as many as he needeth.

THAT STILL, SMALL VOICE.
(Obedience)

    That still, small Voice. You know… the one you hear in the back of your mind, but you choose to ignore it? The one that tells you to go here or go there, to look in this place or that place or somewhere totally unexpected? The one that, when you FINALLY listen to it, you find a solution to your problem?
    Time after time after time, it has happened to me. You would think that, as long as I have been walking with the Lord, I would automatically respond when I hear "that Voice," but my flesh gets in the way and I am slow to listen.
    One of the times that stands out like a neon sign is the time that I had misplaced my gradebook for school, and I desperately needed to find it. I frantically looked everywhere for it, and it was nowhere to be found — bookshelves, in and under my baskets where students turned in their work, in the classroom storage closet, even under my desk where I kept a boxful of miscellaneous stuff. Not a sign of it anywhere!
    Since I lived twenty-five miles from the school I taught at, I was reluctant to go home without it, but I did. After checking my car and my home thoroughly, I accepted the fact that it had to be at school, so I turned around and took my husband with me to go back to look for it.
    That was when that little Voice reminded me, "Look under your desk."
    Being the obedient woman that I am, I mentally replied, "I already looked there."
    But the Voice spoke again. "Look under your desk in the box."
    Once more, I responded that I had looked there.
    Then the Voice became very insistent. "I said LOOK THERE

AGAIN!!!"

Well, the third time was the charm, so I finally paid attention, and after I dug just a little deeper than the surface, there was the gradebook! Then I remembered that I had placed it there for safekeeping, and that is exactly where it was.

Another neon moment has to do with my teaching experience as well. One day when I was getting ready to go home, I couldn't find my car keys. I knew I had them somewhere because I could not have gotten to school without them, but it was a mystery to me as to where I had them this time. Once more, I looked high and low and everywhere in between, and no keys. As before, I even looked in the classroom closet, which I kept locked so sticky fingers wouldn't help themselves to our various treasures — or to my own possessions, like my wallet... or car keys.

I became convinced that they were nowhere to be found, so I called home and asked my husband to bring me the second set of keys so I could go home. Thankfully, he did. And he didn't chastise me for my negligence.

The next day at school, I heard that Voice again.

"Look on the middle shelf in the closet," It said.

After the experience with the gradebook, I wasn't quite so stubborn, so I did as I was commanded. As I opened the closet and moved some of the things around, I saw a glimmer of silver. I dug around a little bit further, and lo and behold — my missing keys!

It still happens, even with being retired. But I think (at least I hope!) I've gotten less headstrong over the years. But now, when I hear that Voice, my attitude is more like, "Speak, Lord. Your servant is listening!"

I really don't like admitting my foibles, but God's great mercies have covered me, and I praise Him alone for His faithfulness. May I always be quick to respond to His leading.

1 Samuel 3:9
Therefore Eli said to Samuel, "Go, lie down; and it shall be, if He calls you, that you must say, 'Speak, Lord, for Your servant hears.'"

Isaiah 30:21
Your ears shall hear a word behind you, saying, "This is the way, walk in it," whenever you turn to the right hand or whenever you turn to the left.

1 Kings 19:12
…But the Lord was not in the earthquake; and after the earthquake a fire, but the Lord was not in the fire; and after the fire, a still small voice.

ROOTS OF THANKFULNESS
(Gratitude)

November is a great time of year to look at how much we have to be thankful for. At the top of my list, I thank God for His goodness to me, not only this year but in past years as well.

I remember a time when my children needed new shoes, but I was willing to settle for new shoelaces. That experience made me thankful for new shoes for my kids and myself that we could buy whenever we needed or even wanted some.

We didn't have running water and I had four little ones, so I really needed water for bathing, for washing dishes, for cooking, for anything that needs running water... I was thankful for the water I carried to my house in jugs. Now I praise God for providing me with a water well that works and all the things I use it for—faucets and showers to turn it off and on. And the hot water that goes with it. And flush toilets.

There was a time when I thought I was living high off the hog when I had $40 for groceries once a month. Now it is not uncommon for me to spend $50 two or three times a week. I do give thanks with a grateful heart for God's provisions.

Believe it or not, one of the things I have been thankful for was the first time I needed to pay taxes. Even though it was something most people would complain about, it meant something entirely different to me... it meant that I actually HAD an income and I was thankful for it.

My list of things to be thankful for grows...

Electricity that doesn't come to my house by way of 200 feet of extension cord... Garbage pickup... A decent vehicle that is not rigged so that it will work... food in my pantry... food for my animals... health insurance... clothes that did not come as hand-me-downs... a steady income, even as a senior citizen.

Like the Apostle Paul in Philippians 4:12, I have learned to be abased or to abound. I must admit it is a whole lot easier to be comfortable when abounding, but the sweetest times in life were the times I was abased. I never, ever want to forget how much I have had to depend on God, no matter what the circumstances are. He has been the Rock on which I stand and I praise Him.

What do you have to be thankful for?

Psalm 35:18
I will give Thee thanks in the great congregation: I will praise Thee among much people.

Psalm 100:4
Enter into His gates with thanksgiving, and into His courts with praise:
Be thankful unto Him, and bless His name.

Psalm 103:2–5
Bless the Lord, oh my soul, and forget not all His benefits:
Who forgiveth all thine iniquities; who healeth all thy diseases;
Who redeemeth thy life from destruction: who crowneth thee with lovingkindness and tender mercies:
Who satisfieth thy mouth with good things so thy youth is renewed like the eagle's.

REDEEMING THE TRASH
(Overcoming Rejection)

I am one of those people who hangs on to a lot of unnecessary stuff and eventually culls it for disposal. Recently I found that quirk to be a blessing. This happened when I was cleaning out what I call "The Land of the Lost," the room where I store things I want but don't necessarily need.

It happened when I was clearing out some old papers and bills from the past. Before something ended up in the pile to be discarded, I carefully looked through each piece and opened each envelope before I put it in the can. One piece in particular caught my attention. It was addressed to my husband and it was from a cell phone company.

My husband had died two years earlier, so I knew he would not be opening it. The envelope felt like it had a credit card offer inside, so my curiosity was aroused. Should I just chunk it or not? I found myself opening the envelope and was totally surprised to find a MasterCard debit card inside for the amount of $46.77, set to expire in August, 2021. Wow! It was like finding money, except I wasn't sure if it would still be valid since he was no longer on earth.

Needless to say, my fat little fingers punched the phone number to the card company as quickly as I could. Yes, I would be able to redeem the card and they told me the steps to take to do it. Thankfully, the process was smoother than I expected and I reaped my husband's harvest for the gift card. I was a little richer because of my find, but I think how easily it would have been just to disregard the envelope addressed to him.

How much like people in general to make judgement on people we come across who seem to be less than perfect?

Some people are thought to be less worthy because of their station, or lack thereof, in life. It would have been so easy for me to trash that envelope, but giving it a deeper look blessed me with an unexpected amount of money.

Think about the waitress at a diner… the sales clerk at a store… the garbage collector… construction workers…the janitor in any business… etc. If we come across someone with a degree of wealth or prestige, do we treat them any differently than we do the people who have the more menial tasks?

The Bible tells us in no uncertain terms not to regard one group of people above other groups.

> **James 2**
> *My brethren, do not hold the faith of our Lord Jesus Christ, the Lord of glory, with partiality.*
> *For if there should come into your assembly a man with gold rings, in [a]fine apparel, and there should also come in a poor man in [b]filthy clothes, and you [c]pay attention to the one wearing the fine clothes and say to him, "You sit here in a good place," and say to the poor man, "You stand there," or, "Sit here at my footstool," have you not [d]shown partiality among yourselves, and become judges with evil thoughts?*

Remember the story of the Rich Man and Lazarus? The rich man's money did nothing to influence God's favor.

> **Luke 16**
> *There was a certain rich man who was clothed in purple and fine linen and he fared sumptuously every day.*
> *But there was a certain beggar named Lazarus, full of sores, who was laid at his gate, desiring to be fed with the crumbs which fell from the rich man's table. Moreover the dogs came and licked his sores.*
> *So it was that the beggar died, and was carried by the*

angels to Abraham's bosom. The rich man also died and was buried.
And being in torments in Hades, he lifted up his eyes and saw Abraham afar off, and Lazarus in his bosom.
Then he cried and said, 'Father Abraham, have mercy on me, and send Lazarus that he may dip the tip of his finger in water and cool my tongue; for I am tormented in this flame.'
But Abraham said, 'Son, remember that in your lifetime you received your good things, and likewise Lazarus evil things; but now he is comforted and you are tormented. And besides all this, between us and you there is a great gulf fixed, so that those who want to pass from here to you cannot, nor can those from there pass to us.'

If you find yourself making judgements on old papers and envelopes, that is one thing and all you may lose is a few dollars. But, on the other hand, if you are showing partiality to people because of their station in life or their monetary worth, you are going against the Word of God.

If you take time to interact with these people, you may be amazed at what they have to offer. Who knows? You may be looking at someone who is a diamond in the rough. And whatever you do, treat them as the Child of God that they are and not as someone who is less than whole. Your encouragement might be the catalyst to help them find their way.

THE BLESSING OF NEW BEGINNINGS
(Overcoming Disappointments)

Where would we be if not for new beginnings? Most of us would be stuck in some horrendous ruts, wishing there were a way out. We would be bemoaning our existence as if complaining would make anything any better. We would never know the joy of leaving the past behind and actually being able to begin again. But thankfully, His mercies are new every morning, and we can start over. And my life has been one of the proofs of that statement over and over and over again.

Becoming a widow in 2019 was not the first time I have had to start over. Once upon a time, I was a divorcée with four little ones, and that definitely was a cause of starting over. But had I not gotten that new beginning, I'm not sure what my life would have been like.

Then there was the time I went back to college to become a teacher well past the age when most of my friends already had careers. With God's help, I started over at age forty-one and taught in public school for the next twenty-four years.

After I retired from teaching, I decided to have a new beginning of my own. I started writing books for publication and actually began a whole new career. One book led to another and to another until I finally had seven publications to my credit—eight if you count the help I gave Helen Colin in writing her autobiography about surviving the Holocaust. I've been blessed with success in more ways than one, in personal sales and new relationships.

My second marriage lasted 39 years, but that is not the end of the story.

Some people will find this hard to believe, but God let me

know ahead of time that a change was on its way. In addition to that, I was told I would "like" what was going to happen. So, a few days later, I wasn't totally caught off guard when I met a man and our lives melded. When God spoke to him and told him, "Take care of Elizabeth," he took it literally and ended up proposing to me less than a month after we met. I accepted. We were married November 6, 2021, and life hasn't been the same since.

Some people may think this is a little too much information—and maybe it is—but I said all that to show that God's mercies are new every day, and we can have new beginnings, no matter what age we are. Don't let age define your abilities or your vision... God doesn't.

> **Lamentations 3:22-24**
> *It is of the LORD's mercies that we are not consumed, because his compassions fail not. They are new every morning: great is thy faithfulness.*
>
> **Psalm 103:11**
> *For as the heaven is high above the earth, so great is his mercy toward them that fear him.*
>
> **Psalm 145:8**
> *The LORD is gracious, and full of compassion; slow to anger, and of great mercy.*
>
> **Revelation 21:5**
> *And he that sat upon the throne said, Behold, I make all things new.*
>
> **Isaiah 43:18-19**
> *Remember ye not the former things, neither consider the things of old. Behold, I will do a new thing...*

THE RITUAL OF CLEAN SHEETS
(Hope)

When I think of preparing for a hurricane, I think of a wonderful, strange ritual my mother had when our family prepared for leaving our home during a hurricane… changing bedsheets before we left for safety. The first time I noticed it was in 1961, when Hurricane Carla was approaching the Texas Gulf Coast, and our family was preparing to go to a community shelter as we anticipated the storm. Mom was obviously pregnant with my baby sister, and Dad decided it would be best for us to go where Mom would have help if she needed it. But before we left, we had to change the bedsheets.

I thought this was really weird. Why change bedsheets or even make the bed if there was a chance that we might have nothing to come home to? It seemed to me to be an exercise in futility. Of course, we always came back to our home, and thankfully, it was intact. But the ritual baffled me until I grew up, and now, I find myself mimicking it, even when I go on a trip.

That September, I discovered that I really liked the feel of clean sheets. As I crawled under the covers, I would bask in the crispness of the clean cloths. I would kick my legs in sheer joy at the feeling of the freshness. I smile even now remembering the experience.

Now that I am an adult, I find myself looking forward to sleeping in clean sheets. If I will be gone from home for a few days, for almost any reason, I'll change the sheets before I leave. I've come to see it as a statement of faith, but also a reward for being faithful: a statement of faith because I believe I would return… and a reward for having done the task of changing the sheets.

How does this relate to inspiration? I've found that clean sheets are inspiring first of all as an act of faith. Putting fresh sheets on the bed is a way of saying, "I look forward to the time I will return." And sure enough, the anticipated return reaffirms faith.

Secondly, the clean sheets can represent the robe of righteousness that we receive when we accept Jesus into our hearts. Before He comes in, our lives are full of sin and confusion of all sorts. But after He has been welcomed into our lives, we are covered with His righteousness.

Yes, I know that is stretching it a bit. But isn't it wonderful that we can be blessed with clean sheets and a reminder of the clean feeling we have when all our sins are washed away?

Have you changed your sheets lately?

Romans 1:17
For therein is the righteousness of God revealed from faith to faith: as it is written, the just shall live by faith.

Isaiah 61:10
I will greatly rejoice in the LORD, my soul shall be joyful in my God; for he hath clothed me with the garments of salvation, he hath covered me with the robe of righteousness, as a bridegroom decketh himself with ornaments, and as a bride adorneth herself with her jewels.

Revelation 19:8
And to her was granted that she should be arrayed in fine linen, clean and white: for the fine linen is the righteousness of saints.

LOCKED DOORS LEAD TO TRUST
(Trusting God)

    Very recently, my daughter had to explain a spiritual truth to me.
    I had gone with a friend to a Bible study. When I got home, our small dog needed to go out. I sat my phone down and the keys to the house and took Liddle Girl out to do her business. It was my plan for us to wait for my husband, who would be coming home very shortly. My plan got shot to pieces when I realized I had locked myself out and had no idea of how we were going to get back in.
    We were new to the area, so I didn't know our neighbors. Our landlord's phone number was in my phone, so I never memorized it. Since my phone was in the house, it would not have done any good anyway.
    Finally, after what seemed like an eternity, my husband came home and tried to rescue us. His efforts were as futile as mine, since he didn't have the owner's number either. So we started to play hopscotch with our phones.
    First, we started by calling a relative in our town who might have the owner's number. He didn't. Then we called a friend who has had contact with the owner. He didn't know the owner's number right off hand either. After a few minutes, the friend gave us what he thought was the owner's number. It turned out to be her husband's phone, and he had to call her to get an answer. Once he got hold of her, he found out how to help us… she had a spare key hidden in the side yard.
    Frantically, we followed her directions to get us out of this predicament. As Randy fiddled with the box to get the key out, I saw the side door to the house and decided to try the

handle. Lo and behold! It worked, and we didn't need the key after all!!!

I knew there was a spiritual lesson here, but I wasn't sure what it was. When I told our comedy of errors to my daughter, she made a couple of observations.

First, just because one door is closed, it doesn't mean He hasn't already opened another one. Secondly, she suggested that God makes a way when there seems to be no way.

Humanly speaking, we were in a pickle until we received help via cell phone. But had we known about the hidden key or the unlocked side door, we could have ended our problem before it got out of hand. Little did we know God had it all under control even before we asked.

Psalm 27:14
Wait on the LORD: be of good courage, and he shall strengthen thine heart: wait, I say, on the LORD.

1 Corinthians 16:9
For a great door and effectual is opened unto me, and there are many adversaries.

Isaiah 43:1
Behold, I am doing a new thing; now it springs forth, do you not perceive it? I will make a way in the wilderness and rivers in the desert.

Colossians 4:3
At the same time, pray also for us, that God may open to us a door for the word.

James 2:26
For as the body apart from the spirit is dead, so also faith apart from works is dead.

Romans 8:28

And we know that for those who love God all things work together for good, for those who are called according to his purpose.

USE UP, REPAIR, MAKE DO, OR DO WITHOUT
(Faithfulness)

Back in my childhood days, my parents taught us to use up, repair, make do, or do without. Looking back now, it is easy to understand that they had lived through the Great Depression and knew all kinds of ways to economize. It became a way of life that taught us to recycle before recycling became popular.

We were taught to use dish towels or cloth towels instead of the expensive paper towels. Bacon grease was saved for flavor for future cooking or maybe even homemade soap. All kitchen scraps were saved for the chickens or maybe a hog we were raising to butcher. To throw real food in the trash was unthinkable!

Back in "the day," Kraft put mayo and Miracle Whip in glass jars. That was a blessing because our mom was diligent to use those jars for her famous pickles. She trained us so well, in fact, that I am still using many of those same jars for pickles I make today.

Jars and dishtowels weren't the only things we recycled... we went so far as to re-use bath water! I'm not sure how the order went, but probably Dad got the fresh water, Mom next, and each of us children were in line for a turn as the tub got grimier. Thankfully, those days didn't last forever, and I don't think my youngest siblings even remember those episodes.

With plenty of cousins and friends, we always had clothes, albeit the clothes had been passed down from previous owners. Some things had already been passed around three or four times before they were finally retired.

All of this makes it sound like we were poor, but we never realized it. Most of the people our family was friends with lived in similar fashion. We were all trusting God to take care of us, and He did.

There are so many examples in life and in the Bible of God taking care of His people. I know in my life He has been faithful to take care of us. And I have no doubt He has taken care of you as well.

Exodus 16:35
And the children of Israel did eat manna forty years, until they came to a land inhabited; they did eat manna, until they came unto the borders of the land of Canaan.

Deuteronomy 8:4
Thy raiment waxed not old upon thee, neither did thy foot swell, these forty years.

Matthew 6:27–29
Which of you by taking thought can add one cubit unto his stature?
And why take ye thought for raiment? Consider the lilies of the field, how they grow; they toil not, neither do they spin:
And yet I say unto you, that even Solomon in all his glory was not arrayed like one of these.

2 Corinthians 5:17
Therefore if any man be in Christ, he is a new creature: old things are passed away; behold, all things are become new.

THE FUTILITY OF VANITY
(Pride)

I broke one of my cardinal rules recently, and it didn't take long for me to remember why I had that rule in the first place—to keep vanity at bay.

I'm one of those women who like to think I am low maintenance. I don't relish shopping for clothes; I'm not a shoe diva; I wear very little makeup; I've never dyed or tinted my hair; and the list of "I don't" goes on. However, I didn't heed my own advice when I decided to have a pedicure and a manicure to get ready for a night out on the town with my hubby. (We were still newlyweds, after all!)

The rose-colored nail polish looked absolutely beautiful when I walked out of the salon, but reality hit quickly. From the first day to the next, little pieces of hot pink color started missing—first from one finger, then from another. I wasn't going to let a little disappointment mess up my day, so I tried to act as though no one else would see the imperfection. Instead of stopping at a little damage, my nails added a few more chips every day. As my nails started growing back, the bottom of each painted nail began to show flesh-colored skin a sliver at a time.

After 2 weeks of slowly watching them shrink, I decided to just get the nail polish remover and put me out of my perceived misery. It took a whole lot less time to take it off than it did to paint it on, and I was glad that I didn't have to worry about causing damage to what had started out as a work of art.

I've always marveled at women who consistently have beautiful hands and nails… I've never been one of them. Then I got to thinking about vanity in general and the things we do to put on "a good front..."

My mother realized she was caught in the trap of vanity when she was in her 60s. Up until then, she had dark black hair and she kept it black for years and years. Then she had an epiphany... her efforts were useless because there was always something there to remind her—her roots. She found freedom when she finally admitted that she didn't have to keep up her charade. Her hair grew out to be a beautiful snowy white, with a few flecks of pepper mixed in. She found life was a whole lot easier when she just let nature take its course.

Vanity is not limited to women. Think of the other kinds of things that men and women do for "vanity's" sake: clothing, cars, housing, hairstyles, electronic gadgets, etc.

When King Solomon wrote Ecclesiastes, he said that everything is vanity. Read that book if you want a real wake-up call, because Solomon, the wisest man in the world, spoke from his own experience. And if and when you get caught up in trying to keep up with the Joneses—whether in possessions or physical looks—just think about Solomon's words: "Vanity of vanities," saith the preacher, "all is vanity."

Psalm 39:5 KJV
Behold, thou hast made my days as an handbreadth; and mine age is as nothing before thee: verily every man at his best state is altogether vanity. Selah.

Psalm 94:11
The LORD knoweth the thoughts of man, that they are vanity.

Psalm 119:37
Turn my eyes from looking at worthless things; and give me life in your ways.

Proverbs 31:30
Charm is deceitful, and beauty is vain, but a woman who fears the LORD is to be praised.

IT ALL DEPENDS ON YOUR PERSPECTIVE
(Outlook)

About 30 years ago, there was a fad going around that people latched on to with great gusto. It started with a picture with unrecognizable designs, but if someone looked at it just right—actually, if they stared at it for quite a while—that picture would transform into something familiar: a herd of elephants, a flock of geese, a family of giraffes, a school of fish.

People bought these pictures on a whim because they enjoyed the challenge, but now, many years later, people have forgotten what the big deal was about those pictures.

Recently, one of my children gave us a strange-looking plaque for the wall. It has some strategically placed pieces of wood that look like hieroglyphics. We knew there had to be a message there. We looked and looked and studied it carefully, and it still looked like a special code. Then, when we stepped back and looked at it from a distance, the whole scene transformed. When our perspective changed, the picture changed. Now, when we look at it the right way, we can see "JESUS." Once we've seen Jesus, we can't 'unsee' Him. He follows us wherever we go.

How often do we make that mistake in everyday life? Things seem to be a jumbled mess. The more we try to straighten it out, the more confusing it becomes. What started out as a little distraction has grown into a mountain of problems. But then Jesus shows up, and our situation clears up. When Jesus is on the scene, everything else seems to fall in place.

1 Corinthians 13:12
For now we see through a glass, darkly; but then face to face: now I know in part; but then shall I know even as also I am known.

Ephesians 5:32
This is a great mystery: but I speak concerning Christ and the church.

Romans 16:25
Now to him that is of power to stablish you according to my gospel, and the preaching of Jesus Christ, according to the revelation of the mystery, which was kept secret since the world began.

IN THE LIGHT OF ETERNITY
(Endurance)

Every once in a while, I come across a challenge that is difficult to face. It's the kind of thing that seems earth-shattering when it happens, and I frantically look for a solution, but solutions are few and far between. But, thank God, I've found my own way to deal with them, and that is by looking at it through the light of eternity.

No, this is not some hocus-pocus mind game, but a way to put things in perspective so they don't consume my time and energy. This is how it works... how is this thing going to affect me next week? In 6 months? A year? 5 years? 10 years?

For example, I wore clunky tennis shoes to my mother's funeral because of having problems with my feet. Protocol would say dress respectfully in honor of the deceased. Practicality, on the other hand, said, "You want to be able to walk without a limp, don't you?"

It seemed like a major faux pas waiting to happen, but in the end, I had to ask myself how this would affect me in eternity. What would this matter in a month? A year? 5 years? Probably no consequence at all. So, I lost the guilt over my choice of footgear, and my feet thanked me for it.

Choices do matter, but not all choices have the same outcome. Some are inconsequential; some have major impact on our lives. I will admit, some things can have major effect on a life, and the outcome will overshadow a life for years to come... the choice of a mate... a career... place to live... lifestyle choices. These are the kinds of things that can make you or break you. But even in those situations, God can help you straighten out what seems like a mess otherwise.

So, when things happen that seem catastrophic at the

time, take time to step into the future so you can look back on them from a different perspective. It may make things easier to deal with.

    Bottom line is: don't major on the minors. Look at the situation through the eyes of eternity. Trust God because He is in control.

> **Proverbs 16:9**
> *In their hearts, humans plan their course, but the LORD establishes their steps.*
>
> **Proverbs 14:12**
> *There is a way that appears to be right, but in the end it leads to death.*
>
> **Deuteronomy 30:19**
> *This day I call the heavens and the earth as witnesses against you that I have set before you life and death, blessings and curses. Now choose life, so that you and your children may live.*

HAPPY BEING ME
(Contentment)

    After years and years of finding fault with myself, I've come to realize that I like being me and having my own set of problems. That may sound arrogant, but it's true.
    It's easy to think that someone else's life is better for whatever reason—money, family, housing, vehicles, etc.—but I can't think of anyone that I would choose to trade places with. On the surface, another person may have more money, but that money comes at a high cost: peace of mind. How often do they have to check the locks on their doors and windows or watch who is following behind? How many friends do they have just because of the size of their bank account? How quickly will the "friends" leave when the finances are gone?
    Housing is just as mercurial. Really nice houses cost more in maintenance, electricity, and aesthetics. A mobile home provides shelter, as does a mansion, and an apartment can provide warmth and protection for hundreds of dollars less as compared to thousands or even millions for luxury living.
    Many people envy the rich and famous, but I'm not one of them. Famous people have lost their personal privacy just because the rest of the population wants to stick their noses in the celebrity's business. What good is it going to do me to try to keep up with trendsetters when I have enough of my own situations to deal with?
    A person may have wealth, but they may also have ulcers to go with it. A couple may look fantastic on the cover of a magazine but have a relationship that is in shambles. A family works to present a perfect persona, but the truth comes out that one of the children is wayward and mom and dad are

in agony over their loss. There are dozens of other scenarios that remind me that I wouldn't want their problems, and I am more than happy just to be me.

1 Timothy 6:6-7
But godliness with contentment is great gain. For we brought nothing into the world, and we can take nothing out of it.

Hebrews 5:13
Keep your lives free from the love of money and be content with what you have, because God has said, "Never will I leave you; never will I forsake you."

Matthew 6:25-26
Therefore I tell you, do not worry about your life, what you will eat or drink; or about your body, what you will wear. Is not life more than food, and the body more than clothes?
Look at the birds of the air; they do not sow or reap or store away in barns, and yet your heavenly Father feeds them. Are you not much more valuable than they?

Philippians 4:11
I am not saying this because I am in need, for I have learned to be content whatever the circumstances.

YOU CAN'T JUDGE A BOOK BY ITS COVER
(Judging Others)

Recently I read the story about a preacher who was new to his congregation. He had not met them previously, so he was able to pull a disguise of sorts.

He dressed down for his first time at the Sunday morning church service in his new position, meaning instead of putting on his Sunday best, he dressed like a derelict and sat outside the church doors. He also wandered around the church grounds, and only 3 of the thousands of congregants even spoke to him. Most members of the fellowship walked past him without acknowledging him. Sometimes they even turned the other way or stopped to stare contemptuously.

He sat at the front of the church when it was time for the service to begin, but the ushers made sure to escort him to the back. After all the preliminaries were complete, the members would greet the new minister—and they did not want that pathetic-looking man getting his attention. Imagine their shock when the homeless man walked to the front and introduced himself as their new leader. It was their wake-up call.

When Jesus came to earth, He gave the world a wake-up call. He was a lot like that preacher. Although He was the King of the Universe, He didn't look the part. People in Israel expected a monarch with earthly power and someone who would overthrow Roman control. What they got instead was a baby born in a barn who was meek and mild and definitely not a politician!

Jesus wasn't recognized as someone special during His time on earth, and His family was concerned that He was mentally unstable. That's why He made the statement that a prophet isn't welcome in his own town. Wherever He went, He was despised and rejected by men.

Sometimes people come into our lives seemingly out of nowhere. They enter without fanfare, work beside us willingly and without trumpets blaring, and return to where they come from just as quietly as they arrived. There may be an air of mystery about them that confuses us. That's when we may realize that person might have been an angelic visitation—something that was not expected.

Think about the child that seemed to lack ability to accomplish almost anything. Or the young mother without a husband and no source of income. Or the down-and-out truck driver who ends up becoming a superstar. Or the quirky teen who becomes a computer guru. And the list goes on and on.

Some people look so incapable of being a success that others are shocked when the odd person succeeds at anything. But God can and does make new creations. He has a plan for everyone's life, and His plans for us are for good, not evil. We can become new creations if we have handed control to the Creator of the Universe.

2 Corinthians 5:17
Therefore, if anyone is in Christ, he is a new creation. The old has passed away; behold, the new has come.

Galatians 6:15
For neither circumcision counts for anything, nor uncircumcision, but a new creation.

Jeremiah 29:11
For I know the plans I have for you, declares the LORD, plans for welfare and not for evil, to give you a future and a hope.

Hebrews 13:2
Do not neglect to show hospitality to strangers, for thereby some have entertained angels unawares.

THE MIRACLE FROM THE TITHE
(Tithing and Giving)

I was a young mother with four lively young 'uns in the early '70s when I first learned of the blessings of tithing. But I had a problem, and it would take a miracle from God Himself for me to be able to tithe. You see, although I was a new believer in the Lord Jesus Christ, I was also in a marriage that was full of strife and discord—and a severe lack of finances.

Nonetheless, I heard about tithing on Christian radio, found the Biblical support for it, and wanted to do my part as a believer. All I needed to do was do it. But how? My husband rarely gave me any grocery money, much less money to do anything else with, so when he gave me $40 for groceries one day in '76, I was so excited that I spent it all on groceries and forgot to keep out the tithe. Now I had to figure out how to make things right, so I started mulling the problem over.

My solution turned out to be quite simple—tithe on the groceries. I contacted a friend and asked her to be my private investigator to find someone with a need. Marleah did as asked and came up with the name of a family who had met hard times financially and had 2 or 3 kids and one on the way (I think that is what happened). They were without groceries till their next paycheck, and I believed God wanted to use me to bless them.

Excitedly, I started grabbing from my groceries and packing in things I thought would bless them—hamburger meat, bread, sugar, eggs, etc.—until I had filled not one, but two bags, much more than 10% of my purchase. Then I asked Marleah to be my go-between, to deliver the goods to them, but not let them know who their benefactor was. Marleah was true to her word, and I felt like I had not let the Lord down after all.

    I forgot about the matter for several months, and then, out of the blue, the couple contacted me. As it turned out, they were getting ready to move and could not take everything with them. Would I be offended if they gave me what was left in their pantry? By this time, they were back on their feet, but my marriage had totally fallen apart and I was having to move closer to my parents, so I readily accepted their offer.

    Laughingly and rejoicing over God's goodness, I shared with them how the Lord had used me in their lives a few months before—and now I was receiving their overflow.

    As I loaded and unloaded their items, I was shocked to find just how much was overflow... between food, clothing, and odds and ends of furniture, toys, and stuff, the total value of everything was well over $200! Not bad for returns on a $4 tithe!!!

    Since that time, I have been a faithful tither as well as a faithful giver. I didn't realize there was a difference between tithing and giving, but now I do, and both are extremely important in God's economy. It's like giving tithes and offerings turns on the faucet so God can pour His blessings out on us. And I know from personal experience—He will never let you down.

> **Malachi 3:9-10**
> *Ye are cursed with a curse: for ye have robbed me, even this whole nation.*
> *Bring ye all the tithes into the storehouse, that there may be meat in mine house, and prove me now herewith, saith the LORD of hosts,*
> *if I will not open you the windows of heaven, and pour you out a blessing, that there shall not be room enough to receive it.*

Malachi 3:8
Will a man rob God? Yet ye have robbed me. But ye say, Wherein have we robbed thee? In tithes and offerings.

Mark 4:24
And he said unto them, Take heed what ye hear: with what measure ye mete, it shall be measured to you: and unto you that hear shall more be given.

Luke 6:38
Give, and it will be given to you. Good measure, pressed down, shaken together, running over, will be put into your lap.
For with the measure you use it will be measured back to you.

Proverbs 3:9
Honor the LORD with your wealth and with the first fruits of all your produce.

2 Corinthians 9:6-7
The point is this: whoever sows sparingly will also reap sparingly, and whoever sows bountifully will also reap bountifully.
Each one must give as he has decided in his heart, not reluctantly or under compulsion, for God loves a cheerful giver.

I REMEMBER GOING BACK TO COLLEGE
(Starting Over)

We were both middle-aged matrons with families to care for and little or no income to speak of. Both of us were friends from as far back as high school in the '60s, and both of us attended Wharton County Junior College many moons ago. Both of us were frustrated with the lack of worldly goods in our lives and the need to use food stamps to get by. And then, seemingly out of the blue, my friend Faye got a harebrained idea. "Liz," she said, "I'm going back to college. Why don't you come, too?"

With five kids at home, a husband with little income, and a food delivery business that was getting nowhere fast, I laughed at the improbability of it all. But then, the words of my college professor, Dr. C.P. Williams, came back to haunt me. He, too, had cajoled me to complete my degree.

"But Dr. Williams," I whined, "I'm 38 years old, and it's been 17 years since I finished WCJC!"

He smiled as he asked, "How old will you be if you do go back to college and get your certification?"

Weakly, I replied, "Forty-one."

"And," he continued, "how old will you be if you DON'T go back?" Since time was going to pass either way, it looked like I might as well do something productive to help improve our situation in life.

So, after immense prayer and soul-searching, I was a student again, juggling classes and carpools to UH–Victoria and family obligations in Wharton.

God must have helped me in my plans the first time around, because all but seven of my 126 credits from the early '70s transferred after the interim. What surprised me was how many other middle-aged mommas and men were also making midlife career changes by going back to school. Although there were many young people enrolled, it seemed that there were just as many of us who were young at heart.

Testing at all the steps along the way was a real nightmare... placement tests, TASP tests, class tests, semester exams, and, finally, ExCET tests. My poor family suffered as their loving, mild-mannered mother became a screaming, temperamental tyrant when it came time to do special reports for classes or to meet certain deadlines for individual teachers.

Finding a compatible carpool was another challenge that weighed heavily in choosing courses each new semester. Although I qualified for Pell Grants and financial aid along the way, I still had to keep up my business and other obligations.

Someone was kind enough to lend me an electric typewriter for my college work. With God's help and abundant grace, I completed my work in about two and a half years. In spite of the struggle and inconvenience, I am so glad that I accepted the challenge.

I used to feel very guilty because I had received many scholarships when I graduated high school in 1969, but didn't follow through on completing my college program. Because of God's help, I believe I have been able to justify and honor the faith that my benefactors had in me, albeit on a delayed basis.

Resuming my education was one of the hardest decisions I have ever made, but one that brings me great pride. Although I considered myself a late bloomer, I am glad to say that I did bloom and brought forth fruit with each and every new school year that I taught.

Isaiah 43:18–19
Remember not the former things, nor consider the things of old. Behold, I am doing a new thing; now it springs forth, do you not perceive it? I will make a way in the wilderness and rivers in the desert.

Proverbs 3:5
Trust in the LORD with all your heart, and do not lean on your own understanding.

Philippians 1:6
And I am sure of this, that he who began a good work in you will bring it to completion at the day of Jesus Christ.

LOOKING AT LIFE FROM GOD'S PERSPECTIVE
(Wisdom/Knowledge)

If you have ever flown in an airplane or helicopter, you've noticed how things on earth diminish in size as you go higher and higher. Eighteen-wheelers become like grains of rice; people walking around look like ants; city lights twinkle like fireflies on a summer night; rivers and streams twist and turn on the ground like pieces of ribbon. Whatever way you are going causes the scene to go from bigger to smaller, or smaller to bigger, depending on your altitude.

That's the way our lives should be with God. Viewing life situations from His elevation helps us see more clearly. It's then that we realize maybe our problems are not as unsurmountable as we thought.

There was no way that a shepherd boy could bring down a giant the size of Goliath without divine intervention, but he had God on his side, and he won the victory.

> **Romans 8:31–33**
> *What shall we then say to these things? If God be for us, who can be against us?*

How about Gideon's army? The Lord kept whittling and whittling down until there were only 300 soldiers left. The odds weren't very good, but God plus one equals a majority. The Israelis ended up whooping their enemies because of God.

What if you don't think your faith is strong enough to overcome obstacles? That was the challenge a father had for his son who was deathly ill. But Jesus reassured him that healing and restoration were possible.

Mark 9:24
"And straightway the father of the child cried out, and said with tears, Lord, I believe; help thou mine unbelief."

Even King David, a man after God's own heart, had doubts about his own abilities when he realized his own insignificance.

Psalm 22:6
But I am a worm, and no man; a reproach of men, and despised of the people.

Don't give up on yourself because your life doesn't fit a certain mold. Maybe God will use you to start something new. Trust Him for direction. He loves you and will not let you go.

Zechariah 4:10
For who hath despised the day of small things? for they shall rejoice...

Romans 8:28
We know that God causes everything to work together for the good of those who love God.

1 John 5:14
And this is the confidence that we have in him, that, if we ask anything according to his will, he heareth us

Mark 9:23
Jesus said unto him, If thou canst believe, all things are possible to him that believeth.

SYNCHRONIZED FLYING AND OTHER MARVELS OF NATURE

So many things in nature seem to be random in the way they act and react, but that is not always the case. Some Master Designer has orchestrated the whole shebang, and it is awesome to watch. For example, birds when they demonstrate synchronized flying.

I've been fascinated watching birds in flight. So often they create a moving panorama that changes from one instance to the next. No choreographer could produce masterpieces like these, yet nature puts on a show when grackles fly to feed in the fields for a day or to fly to their roosts.

Grackles aren't the only entertainers. Birds that live by the seashore are just as talented as they skim above the waves or go looking for their next handout. So are geese in their V-shape formations.

Nature is full of creative organisms. Watch a colony of ants one day and try to figure out which one is the leader. They work together without a rebellion, and they get the job done. Or a cloud of grasshoppers or locusts? They move in unison without having anyone in charge. If humans worked with that kind of harmony, we could lay down the weapons of war.

Once upon a time, I had a cage with several pairs of doves nesting in it. I delighted in watching a momma and a daddy take turns feeding the hungry babies. Daddy did as much to care for them as Momma did, and caring for their little ones was their main goal in life. (Side note—on a 4th of July several years ago, I opened the door and gave them their freedom. For a long time after that, several doves would fly past my head as if to say 'Thank you!')

The Bible says we can learn from the animals. Maybe now is the time we should.

Job 12:7-10
But ask the animals, and they will teach you, or the birds in the sky, and they will tell you;
or speak to the earth, and it will teach you, or let the fish in the sea inform you.
Which of all these does not know that the hand of the Lord has done this?

Jeremiah 8:7
Even the stork in the sky knows her appointed seasons, and the dove, the swift, and the thrush observe the time of their migration. But my people do not know the requirements of the Lord.

Job 35:11
Who teaches us more than he teaches the beasts of the earth and makes us wiser than the birds in the sky?

Proverbs 6:6-8
Go to the ant, you sluggard; consider its ways and be wise!
It has no commander, no overseer or ruler,
yet it stores its provisions in summer and gathers its food at harvest.

Psalm 8:6-9
You made them rulers over the works of your hands; you put everything under their feet:
all flocks and herds, and the animals of the wild,
the birds in the sky, and the fish in the sea, all that swim the paths of the seas.
Lord, our Lord, how majestic is your name in all the earth!"

Proverbs 30:24-28

There are four things which are little on the earth, but they are exceedingly wise:
the ants are a people not strong, yet they prepare their food in the summer;
the rock badgers are a feeble folk, yet they make their homes in the crags;
the locusts have no king, yet they all advance in ranks;
the spider skillfully grasps with its hands, and it is in kings' palaces.

FROM MY HEAD TO MY HEART
(Testimony)

I've done a lot of traveling since November 2021, more than I had ever even thought about in the previous 70 years of my life. I've been to more than 20 states and 3 foreign countries with my husband Randy, and we have enjoyed it all. We have travelled by car and truck and airplane, and we've stayed in hotels, motels, friends' homes, church camps, and RV camps. It's totaled thousands of miles, and I will probably add a few thousand more before my life is over.

But out of all my travels, the one journey that has the only lasting effect was the shortest... the 18 inches from my head to my heart. That's when my knowledge of Jesus went from my head to my heart in 1974.

I prided myself on being a really good person, even though I had defied my parents in order to marry a man who was a horrible prospect for the future. I thought he needed me to help him get his life in order. That was before I found out that Jesus saves, and I couldn't. My life was miserable, and my 2 babies were suffering too—plus I had one on the way. I wanted a way out, and I needed a Savior. That was when I surrendered my life to the control of the Master, and He took over.

It's difficult for a self-righteous person to admit need for someone to save them. It's even more difficult for that kind of person to acknowledge that he or she is a sinner. But that is exactly what I did when my soul took that 18-inch journey.

I had lots of head knowledge about the Bible, about spiritual things, and about Heaven. However, it had not gone to the depths of my soul. That was about to change...

I was home alone with my little ones when the Holy Spirit

nudged my heart by way of the **700 Club**. I knelt by the side of a chair in our living room and prayed with show host Pat Robertson.

"Lord," I said, "I'd like to think I'd go to Heaven if I died, but I'm not so sure I would. Please forgive me of my sins and come live in my heart. I love You, Lord, and I want to be Yours for all eternity."

That's when my life took a new direction. Although I didn't see it physically, I changed—even though my situation didn't.

I could deal with heartache and neglect. I learned to be content with what I had. I realized that God was concerned about me and my children even if my husband wasn't. I trusted in my Heavenly Father's care, and I knew that I knew that I knew everything was going to be all right. His peace flowed like a river, and I am forever grateful.

My spiritual journey began when what I knew about Jesus in my head sank down to my heart.

Have you made that journey too?

> **Isaiah 43:18**
> *Remember not the former things, nor consider the things of old.*
>
> **Isaiah 43:19**
> *Behold, I will do a new thing; now it shall spring forth; shall ye not know it? I will even make a way in the wilderness, and rivers in the desert.*
>
> **John 3:3**
> *Jesus answered and said unto him, Verily, verily, I say unto thee, Except a man be born again, he cannot see the kingdom of God.*
>
> **2 Corinthians 5:17**
> *Therefore if any man be in Christ, he is a new creature: old things are passed away; behold, all things are become new.*

MOMENTS OF
SERENDIPITY

ABOUT THE AUTHOR

Elizabeth Dettling Moreno was born in Wharton, Texas, in 1950. She was the third child of six born to John and Geraldine Wendel Dettling, three girls and three boys.

Moreno is the author of the children's picture book *Sancho, the Silly Billy Goat*, and *The Return of Sancho, the Not So Silly Billy Goat*, plus the chapter book, *Tales from the Chicken Yard and Other Fowl Stories*. She has also published three coloring books and helped Holocaust Survivor Helen Colin write her autobiography, *My Dream of Freedom, from Holocaust, to my beloved America*.

    She wrote her own autobiography in *Psalms of Motherhood and Other Reflections on Life*. It chronicles the struggles of her first marriage and how the Lord took care of her and her 4 children after the divorce. It also sheds light on the blessings that the Lord bestowed on her and her children as she learned to walk by faith and not by sight. She did get married a second time and added another child. That marriage lasted 39 years until her husband died from kidney disease in 2019. But that wasn't the end of her story.

After 2 years of being a widow, God brought Randy Tolman into her life and they married in November, 2021. One of the first things they did was begin a ministry they call "Life After Death." As of March, 2025, they have traveled to more than 22 states and 3 foreign countries. They have a unique story about how God brought them together to share their lives in marriage.

www.ingramcontent.com/pod-product-compliance
Lightning Source LLC
LaVergne TN
LVHW061038070526
838201LV00073B/5097